Carrie Jenkins Harris

Mr. Perkins, of Nova Scotia

Or, The European Adventures of a would-be Aristocrat

Carrie Jenkins Harris

Mr. Perkins, of Nova Scotia
Or, The European Adventures of a would-be Aristocrat

ISBN/EAN: 9783337067588

Printed in Europe, USA, Canada, Australia, Japan

Cover: Foto ©ninafisch / pixelio.de

More available books at **www.hansebooks.com**

Mr. Perkins, of Nova Scotia;

—OR—

THE EUROPEAN ADVENTURES OF A WOULD-BE ARISTOCRAT.

—BY—

CARRIE J. HARRIS,

WOLFVILLE, N. S.

WINDSOR, N. S.
J. J. ANSLOW, BOOK, NEWSPAPER & GENERAL JOB PRINTER.
1891.

Entered according to Act of the Parliament of Canada, in the year 1891, by CARRIE J HARRIS, *at the Department of Agriculture.*

MR. PERKINS, OF NOVA SCOTIA.

CHAPTER I.

Lights streamed from every window of Chestnut Villa one memorable evening during the month of December, 1889. Inside the mansion, all was bustle and confusion, for, on the morrow, the youngest son, the pride and hope of the Perkinses, was about to add to the family lustre, by starting on a grand European tour.

"A trip to Europe! Just think of it," remarked the eldest daughter of the house when the subject was first discussed. "Why, mamma, we shall be the envy and admiration of the whole community! Just think what glowing accounts Thomas Obadiah can write home to us; we will need no other entertainment for our guests between the dances, when we give our balls this winter, and when Janie Maud and I go out into society, we will always have something to talk about. We can tell our partners what he sees in Europe, for you know he can write such beautiful letters, so full of sentiment and poetry."

"Wa-al, I do declare, Julie Ann?" remarked the young lady's papa; "Wa-al, I do declare! I did not know that you was in need of anything to talk about when you go a visiting; you generally manage to make your tongue run fast enough to home."

"Oh, papa, you do not, of course, understand! One always needs a subject for conversation in society. And do not, for goodness sake, call me Julie Ann! It does sound so plebeian! By my family, and very particular friends, I wish to be addressed as Julia Anna. Although I must confess that Jule has a poetical sound, yet I have a weakness for two names, and I do not think that Jule Anna makes a graceful combination."

"Poetical fiddlesticks! Your ma was always called Julie Ann, and I guess what's good enough for her is good enough for you! You will never make such butter and shortcake as she used to make. Why, when we were first married, she used to keep the hull house up with her butter and eggs. She would lay down the eggs in—"

"Janie Maud! Janie Maud!" cried a voice from the depths of the sofa; "Open the window quickly, I am fainting! Hand me a glass of water, Julia Anna, please; your papa is so coarse; he has no respect whatever for my nerves."

"Wa-al there, ma, I'll shet up. I guess you feel better now, and we'll talk about this tower acrost the Atlantic for Tom. How much do you s'pose it will cost? Heaps of money, of course."

"Oh, of course it will be quite expensive, but I suppose you are already aware that no young man of culture at the present day settles down to a profession without first taking a trip to Europe."

"Wa-al, I don't know about that. Dave Holmes ain't a bad doctor, and he hasn't tripped to Europe yet."

"The Holmeses are not people of wealth and distinction, like ourselves."

"Ain't, hey? I've seen the time I was mighty glad to git twenty cents a day from them for weeding turnips and sech like, when I was a boy to home."

"Julia Anna, hand me a fan, please!"

"Wa-al, I'll shet up and stick to the tower, but you do rile me so with your airs, you and the gals, since we got rich, that it's a rale pleasure to bring up old—what do you call them, Julie?"

"I presume you mean reminiscences, papa."

"Yes, likely that's the word. We'll say so, anyhow. I don't understand much of this new-fangled talk that you have all got hold of lately."

"I am afraid, papa," now remarked the youngest daughter, "that if we spend the morning in such useless talk as this, poor Thomas will not be ready to start when the next steamer sails, and we all very much wish him to sail in her, for an English family of wealth and distinction, who have been travelling in America, are returning home on board."

"Wa-al, what's Tom to do with that business?" Still, if he wants to go, I'll put up a thousand dollars to settle his hash."

"To defray his expenses, you mean, I presume. Well, I think, that by practising the most strict economy, he might manage with that sum."

"Yes, I have no doubt that he will have to be awful economical, but it's all he's a-going to git from me to waste this year, you may bet your old boots. So there now! But plan away amongst yourselves; it's time I was gitting to work. It won't pay having a lot of men idling around till all hours in the morning, and Bill ain't no good unless he's looked after."

"Our son William never forgets that he is a gentleman."

"No, nor don't intend to let any one else, if he can help it."

"Do you not think, papa, that it would sound better if you were to say that you were going out to superintend your workmen? What would some of our friends think if they were to hear you say that you actually took those awful implements in your hand, with which it is necessary to be familiar in order to practice the profession of agriculture?"

"Those awful implements, as you call them, have often been handled by your old dad, and would still have to be most of the time in his hands if he had not made a lucky hit with potatoes and apples a few years ago; and you, instead of wiping the parlor floors with your long-tailed silks and satins, would have to be in the pantry spatting butter at this time, or doing your own washing, like your mother did afore you. But I must git, or I will soon have to bring a bucket of water to fetch you all out of fainting fits."

"Oh, dear!" said Julia, as her father left the room; "I quite despair of ever being able to tone papa down and make a gentleman of him."

"Your papa, my dears," replied her mother, "is the rough diamond. He is one of Nature's gentlemen. It will take years of polishing to make him perfect, but he is none the less valuable because unpolished. Now, girls, summon Thomas Obadiah and William to the family conclave, and let us decide about this European tour at once."

"Here they are! Oh, boys, at what an opportune moment you have arrived."

"What does the pater say about my proposed holiday? That is the most momentous question with me at the present moment," asked the younger son.

"He says, my dear boy," replied his mother, "that he will give you a thousand dollars to defray your expenses. Do you think you can manage with that sum?"

"If I cannot, I suppose that he will hand over more when the time comes."

"I do not think so, for he was very decided on that point, and you know what he is when once he makes up his mind to anything. But I may be able to help you some out of my private purse. And now, Thomas Obadiah—"

"Drop the Obad, please; I am not particularly fond of the second appellation. Thomas O. will pass on paper, but in addressing me verbally, I think Thomas will do very well without any further embellishment."

"Thomas, then, let it be for the future. When do you wish to start?"

"I should like to be ready in about a fortnight, if we can manage it. I will have to take a run down to Halifax and order my outfit, for I do not think the local lights could make a fit perfect enough to suit the fastidious eyes of the Parisians. I think I can manage with four extra suits, with what I already possess. I suppose I ought to have a valet on a tour of this kind, but I do not know where to obtain the proper sort of a person to fill the position. It would not do to have any one belonging around here. If Will did not look so much like me, I might take him along, thus giving him the benefit of the 'grand tour,' as well as keeping the money in the family, as *mon pere* would observe."

"Oh, Thomas!" said Julia admiringly, "How beautifully you do quote French! You are just the one to sustain the family honor by travelling extensively."

"Many thanks, my *carus frater*," replied William, but I have no desire to brush your clothes and comb your hair for you, even to sustain the family honor, as Julia puts it; and now, if you can spare my vote from this precious council, I will say *bon jour*, for I have an engagement to drive Ted Holmes down to the pond this morning. Let me know when you intend to leave on your tour, so that I can have a sufficiently imposing turn-out to start you on your glorious career."

"I declare, mamma," said Julia, as her brother left the room; "William is almost as bad as papa, only his language and manners are more refined. He always has to indulge in sarcasm on every occasion."

"Yes, my dear; but he is an ornament to society for all that, and, I notice, a general favorite with all

You know he is the local reporter, and he will be so flattered that it will appear in the first issue."

"I will think about it, but I must confess that I do not like the idea of inviting him to the house, for he dares to admire Janie Maud."

"Well, mamma, you need have no fears of my admiring Marston, for I have set my heart on the English lord that Thomas is to bring home for me."

"That is right, I am glad to find that you are so sensible! Well, as we now have it all settled, let us go to work and get out the invitations for the party."

CHAPTER II.

"A party, hey? To announce the departure of Tom! It seems to me that you take a mighty sight of trouble. All the English families settled around here will be bothering him with bundles to take home to their friends; if I was him I would slip off quiet, like."

"If there were any persons of distinction among them, it would be a good introduction for him; but I think the greater part of the English around here belong to the middle class, they are all associated with trade in some way."

"I suppose you do not call selling potatoes and fat cattle trade, Mrs. Perkins?"

"Of course not; we quite frequently hear of a British peer selling his prize cattle, and who would have the audacity to say they were connected with trade!"

"You may, I am not much in the way of hearing what the British peers do, myself, I have too much to do, to study the subject, but I call a bargain a bargain, if it's made by a king or a clown."

"To return to my subject, I wish to inform you that the girls must have new dresses for this party, for I intend it to be as select as it can be made around here."

"Humph! what a pity you could not import a few British peers for the occasion, it would give such a tone to the entertainment. But new dresses, hey? It seems to me they need new dresses mighty often. It was only a short time ago that I put up fifty apiece to buy them new silks for the Smith's ball, and I bet they haven't been on their backs since. Wa-al, gals, how much do you want this time? Another hundred, I s'pose. I must give it to you, but it's all you are going to git from me this winter for finery. This tower is a-going to take all my spare cash for this year. When your ma was married she had a gray silk, and she wore it to all the parties that she was invited to for years; now you think a new silk can only be worn a few times. But go, buy your silks, and be happy to this precious party."

The invitations for the party were all sent out, the Saratogas were packed, and the memorable evening had arrived. It wanted but a few minutes of the time appointed for the arrival of the guests when the lady of the house left her dressing-room, and descended the stairs with a stately step. She was dressed in a perfectly-fitting golden-brown satin, with cream lace at her throat and wrists, while an artistic arrangement of the same kind of lace crowned her head. She smiled sweetly upon her husband, who was standing by the steam radiator in the lower hall.

"Why, Robert," she asked, as she drew on her cream kids; "are you not going to dress? The guests will soon begin to arrive."

"Wa-al, no, I guess not to-night. The fact is, I feel kind of tired like, and don't feel like gitting into rigimentals. I will soon go to bed, as I will want to be around early in the morning. Will the gals soon be down? I want to see how fine they look in their new silks. You look mighty fine yourself to-night, ma; you didn't get a new dress too, did you?"

"No," replied his wife, with a pleased smile, for it was something new for her husband to notice her attire; "I did not think it worth while for me to get a new dress to wear at home. With the girls it is different. I only got this a short time ago to wear at Mrs. Jones' reception. Has the mail arrived?"

"Wa-al, yes, there's a paper and a lot of letters on the table for you. I did not know you kept up such a writing with your folks."

"They are probably answers to invitations for the party," she answered, as she sauntered leisurely to the table and began to look over the mail, just as the girls appeared.

"How do you think we look, papa?" asked Julia.

"Fine as fiddles! But why in the name of common sense couldn't you have told me that you didn't have money enough to buy whole dresses; I wouldn't have minded a few dollars more to cover your backs all over. If you didn't have cloth enough, I should have thought that you could have done better without them long tails than go without waists."

"Why, papa, do you not know that our dresses are made in the latest style?"

"Style, hey! Wa-al, all I've got to say is, that it ain't much of a style. I like to see young women decently covered, myself. You would be in a pretty bad pickle if one of them little strings on your shoulder should happen to give way, and your dress dropped off while you was a scurrying around in some feller's arms; I guess your ma would have a worse fainting fit than she does when I begin to talk about the butter and eggs she used to sell. Wa-al, if you are all a-going to be rigged like that, I guess I'll go to bed. I went to a circus once, where there was a lot of young women making exhibitions of themselves, but they wasn't as bad as you, for they all wore tights to cover their nakedness. Be careful not to stand around in the cold half clothed! Good night."

"Good night, papa," sweetly chorused his daughters, well pleased, as their father knew, to see him take himself out of the way before the arrival of the guests.

"One of you girls look over the paper and see what it says about Thomas going to Europe, while I read the letters," called Mrs. Perkins from the upper end of the hall, as her husband disappeared.

Julia quickly opened the paper and turned to the personals. The first paragraph that met her eye ran thus:—

"We understand that our esteemed townsman, Mr. Thomas Obadiah Perkins, intends skating over the duck pond as soon as he is fitted for the performance."

"The mean, contemptible sneak!" exclaimed the elder lady. "Girls, do not either of you dare to dance with Marston to-night, and I will give him so cold a welcome that he will be glad to retire before he is here long. Skating over the duck pond, indeed! What does the fool mean by that?"

"I think it is a slang term used when speaking of crossing the Atlantic," answered her daughter.

"Well, we do not use slang here, nor recognize those who do. For the future, I wish you to drop the acquaintance of the Marstons; they always were a low-minded set, at best, and now we will see who is coming this evening."

With those words Mrs. Perkins broke the seal

of an envelope and read:—"Mr. Marston regrets that he cannot accept Mrs. Perkins' invitation for Monday evening."

"There is no explanation given, it is almost as insulting as the duck pond."

"Why, mamma!" exclaimed Janie Maud, looking over the pile of envelopes, and taking up a huge yellow one, "this surely is not from one of our guests."

"Of course not, look at the superscription. I will tell you, it is from papa's old aunt, down in Guysborough."

"Yes, that's the postmark."

"Throw it into the fire," suggested Julia.

"No, toss it into the table drawer, and I will read it at my leisure. Your papa would never forgive me if I burnt it before it was read."

Just then a peal at the door bell sent the trio into the reception-room, and the business of reading the notes was postponed for a more convenient season.

CHAPTER III.

In about an hour the house was pretty well filled, and all was going merry as a marriage bell, when Mrs. Perkins appeared before Julia, who was floating around in a dreamy waltz, with her most favoured admirer.

"Julia Anna, ask Mr. Smith to excuse you, I want you at once."

"What is the matter, mamma?" asked that young lady, as she followed her parent, with considerable annoyance visible on her fair face.

Her mother merely replied by pointing to the centre of the drawing-room, where she perceived one of the most peculiar looking individuals it had ever been her fate to behold. The figure was clothed in a short, rusty black skirt and gay plaid shawl. Her head was adorned with a bonnet bearing a striking resemblance to a huge coal-hod. Who could it be that her mother would allow to enter the drawing-room at such a time? She first thought

that it was some gipsy fortune-teller who had been
secured for the evening's entertainment; but no,
her mother was too much annoyed by her guest's
appearance to admit of this solution of the difficulty.

"This is my daughter, Julia Anna," said her
mother, by way of introduction.

The stranger rushed towards her, and nearly
smothered her in a gigantic embrace, at the same
time administering a sounding smack on either
cheek, making her tremble for the artistic work
which had been prepared so carefully an hour or
two before; but the first words sounded a death-
knell to all happiness for the rest of the evening.

"So this is my little niece, Julie Annie, that I
used to toss up and down in my arms nearly thirty
years ago! Well, you have growed, to be sure; but
you still keep your good looks, in spite of the fact
that you will soon be an old maid. Why in the
world didn't you git married before this? I am
sure you are pretty enough, and your pa rich, too.
I should have thought you would have lots of
chances; but, child, you need not have been in such
a hurry to welcome your poor old auntie, that you
run down without your waist on. You wasn't
a-going to bed, was you, with a house full of company? Perhaps you are like your pa, don't care
for company; your ma tells me he has gone to bed.
But there, child, I am chattering and keeping you
standing in the cold without your dress on, and

some young man might come in here, too. Let me put my shawl around you. There now, you look more comfortable; run away to bed."

Instead of being grateful for her aunt's solicitude, Julia angrily threw the shawl on the floor, muttering, "You have mussed my dress," and passed swiftly from the room.

"Well, to be sure, she ain't a-going through the hall agin in that plight, is she, Julie Ann?" the old lady asked of Mrs. Perkins.

"Oh, yes! they are all dressed that way here; but I am neglecting my duties as hostess. Let me help you up stairs with your things. You must be so tired after your journey, but I thought you would like to see the girls before going to bed. I will send your tea to your room."

"I am not a bit tired, and will come down and see the folks as soon as I brush my hair and put my cap on. If I had my trunk I would put on my new black silk, but it will be too late for me to git that to-night, as the boys won't want to leave their company and go to the station, but this will do very well. I'll go down into the kitchen and git a cup of tea for myself. Don't you leave the folks any longer, I have some nice fried-cakes in my bag, and will do very well. I got a new silk three years ago to wear to little Alice's wedding. She made such a grand match that we all had to dress fine to go to her wedding."

"Alice did well when she married? I am glad to hear it."

"Yes, she married parson Goudey's son, he was always a likely chap. He gits big pay working in the cotton mills over in Boston. When Alice was home last summer she had four bran new dresses all made in the latest style by a Boston dressmaker. I tell you she made the country folks stare, when she come into meeting the first Sunday after she come down. There, you run right down stairs, I'll come soon. I s'pose the folks will soon be going."

"No, they will not go for hours yet, so take a good long rest before you join us."

Mrs. Perkins was in hopes that the old lady would, in taking a rest, fall asleep; but she was doomed to be disappointed, for a few minutes afterwards she joined her in the drawing-room, where she inflicted a series of tortures on that poor lady that well nigh drove her frantic. She soon found that it was useless for her to take refuge in a fainting fit,—the most effectual way of silencing her husband when he approached a disagreeable subject, —for, instead of quieting the old lady, she immediately began relating her experience of sundry females down in Guysborough, among them parson Goudey's daughter, who married Jacob Brown, and who always required a strong solution of camphor, or some other equally powerful drug, held to her nose before she would recover.

At last the evening was over. The last guests had taken their departure, followed by the injunction to be sure and come to see her if they ever came down to Guysborough. The departure of the guests also relieved the family of her presence, for, thoroughly tired, she had mounted the stairs as soon as the front door was closed.

"Well, girls," said William, when the family found themselves alone, "don't you think that Tom's departure was announced in grand style to-night? It is not everybody that can produce such a curiosity at a ball for the entertainment of their guests. I wonder if there are many more like her down in Guysborough. I sincerely hope that there are not many more like her in the Perkins family. She is going to Boston from here to visit niece Alice. If I had niece Alice's address I should warn her to move, in case she might have as pleasant a surprise as we have had to-night. Oh, she will furnish a delicious dish for many a breakfast table this morning. I had a strong notion of trying to give mother a rest by asking the old girl to waltz with me, only I had a mortal horror of parson Goudey's views on the subject of waltzing. Well, Tom, old boy, I think we had better cram her into the coach and tote her along with us in the morning, if she can stand the fatigue after all she has gone through to-night. I think I need a trip somewhere, and will escort the old girl to Boston in a day or two. In the meanwhile we will let the pater look after her, except when she is needed to help entertain the party callers. Well, I feel tired enough to rest, so will take myself away to bed. I cannot do without my beauty sleep; am like the dear old lady from Guysborough in that respect. I must get that new black silk from the station in the morning to deck her comely person. I wonder if it is as full a dress as Josiah Allen's wife wore at Miss Flann's lawn party in Saratoga? She seems to have as holy a horror of the present fashion of ball-dresses as that august lady. I feel like agreeing with her in that. I wonder if we have many more points in common. Good-night all—or, rather, good-morning"

CHAPTER IV.

THE morning of the departure dawned fair and bright. The whole household at the Perkinses, including the ancient aunt, notwithstanding the fatigues of the previous evening, was astir at an early hour. Mr. Perkins warmly welcomed the aunt, who had laid the foundations of his fortunes. He had been deeply provoked at the innocent cause of their suffering the evening before. Although he often enjoyed a laugh at their expense, when he saw their ridiculous attempts to lead the community in which they lived, on the strength of their sudden accession to fortune a few years before, he by no means liked the idea of having them held up for the ridicule of their acquaintances by another, even though that other was the one to whom they were at first indebted for their prosperity. When she declared her intention of going with the family to the station, Mr. Perkins interfered.

"You must be tired, my dear aunt, after your journey," he said in answer to her appeal: "So you must stay to home with me and let the rest go. There is not room in the carriage for all. I will take you for a drive this afternoon, and show you the improvements in our place since you was here before."

All the *elite* of the little community in which they lived were at the station to see the show, as young Marston remarked to a companion. Mrs. Perkins had decided that it would be best for Julia and Janie Maud to accompany their brother as far as the steamer, and remain in the city until after their aunt's departure for Boston, which William declared should take place at an early day. Mrs. Perkins and William took an affectionate farewell of the young tourist and stepped from the train, the lady calling out as she walked, to be sure and write from all points of interest along the route, and not forget to send her a good description of Paree. As the train moved out from the station, there arose a deafening cheer from the crowded platform.

"In honor of our distinguished traveller, at the outset of his journey," said young Marston; "It will cause him to think kindly of old Nova Scotia while in foreign parts, if he knows our good wishes follow him, and now, boys, as we are about it, three cheers for the old lady from Guysborough. May success attend her journey to and from Boston!"

This was too much for Mrs. Perkins, who, forgetting her dignity, bolted for the carriage, and was driven rapidly from the spot.

On reaching home, she found a complete revolution had taken place in the kitchen. Aunt Deborah was left in undisturbed possession, while the two girls were busily engaged in packing their trunks upstairs. After a good deal of coaxing, and many promises of no further interference from the offending party, the girls were prevailed upon to return to their work, while the old lady went upstairs to unpack and display the new black silk. As soon as dinner was over she was taken for the promised drive, and her poor tortured niece settled down for a quiet afternoon.

For the next few days Mr. Perkins kept her amused, and out of his wife's way, by driving her around the country, and "seeing the sights," as the old lady remarked.

On Monday William announced his intention of going to Boston on the following Wednesday, proposing to take her to spend that day with an old schoolmate, as he would have no other opportunity. His aunt readily swallowed the bait, and prepared for her visit, also informing him that she would go along to Boston with him, as it was much handier travelling with a man than poking around alone.

She returned, tired, at night, and retired early, in order to get up in time to have all her packing done in the morning. She wished to devote the afternoon, to her niece, who, she seemed to think, had been neglected during her visit.

The afternoon proved a stormy one, and poor Mrs. Perkins began to breathe freely once more, as the shades of night were falling. But alas! for human hopes; just before tea a merry peal of sleigh bells came ringing up the drive, and a couple of the Perkins' most aristocratic friends were announced.

"My dear Mrs. Perkins!" exclaimed Miss Smith, one of the most gushing belles of a neighbouring town, "Pray, do not think we are crazy to come out in all this storm, but we could not resist the temptation of taking advantage of the first sleighing of the season. We were so sorry that we could not get down to your charming party: I heard you had such a lovely time." (The last was said with a little spice of malice, which even Mrs. Perkins could not fail to perceive.) "And where are Julia and Janie? I suppose that Thomas has sailed before this time. I wish I were in his place, going to Paris for the winter; but papa says that both Maud and myself shall certainly visit that renowned city some day."

In this way the young lady kept chattering for some time, endeavoring to take up all Mrs. Perkins' attention, leaving the coast clear for her sister to draw out the old fossil, as they afterwards expressed it, when relating the visit to their friends. But at length Miss Maud, who had been shaking with suppressed merriment for some time, could contain herself no longer, and burst into a peal of hearty laughter, drawing the attention of the other occupants of the room to the corner where she had button-holed the old lady.

Although the evident embarrassment of their hostess in no wise disconcerted the young ladies, they soon took their departure. What the entertainment had been for Miss Maud, Mrs. Perkins had no means of knowing; but, judging from the peals of laughter which came floating back to her from the sleigh as it disappeared from view, filled with a number of gay pleasure-seekers, who had been waiting outside while their companions made a party call, she knew it must have been of a very amusing nature, but whatever had been said was the last straw for the poor camel's back. She felt it would be impossible to face her tormenter again, so, pleading a headache, she retired to her room, from which she only emerged a few minutes before it was time for her guest to leave for the station the following morning.

A telegram was sent to her daughters as soon as their aunt departed, and the next evening they arrived to comfort their poor, afflicted mother. Mr. Perkins astonished them all by giving his sympathy in the form of a check for a large amount.

In a few days William returned from Boston, and the family settled down at home to get what amusement could be obtained from a long country winter, where we will leave them to follow the fortunes of Master Thomas across the Atlantic.

CHAPTER V.

On ordinary occasions, when any member of the Perkins family visited the metropolis, they took up their abode at the house of a friend ; but this, certainly, could not be considered an ordinary occasion, for, was not one of the family starting for Europe? Not a member of the community in which they lived had ever crossed the Atlantic for pleasure ; so, as a matter of course, the first hotel of the city was the proper place for them.

On reaching the depot, a cab was called and ordered to the Waverley. After dinner a note was sent to a few of their most intimate friends, asking them to come down on board of the steamer, with the girls, to see Thomas off.

At three a gay party of seven young ladies accompanied him to the pier, where lay the good ship *Vancouver*. The decks were crowded with the passengers and their friends, and a busy scene was presented. The officers were giving orders in the tone that nautical officers always use on the deck of a vessel, while the sailors sprang forward to do their bidding with that alacrity which none except sailors ever seem to consider necessary.

A short time after our friends arrived, the visitors were all ordered ashore. Good-byes were quickly exchanged, and the greater part of the crowd passed from the ship to the pier. The pilot took charge of the *Vancouver*, her moorings were cast off, her head swung slowly around, and she moved majestically out to sea. Thomas was fairly afloat, and the great European tour had commenced.

Julia and Janie Maud watched their brother as long as he was visible on the deck of the steamer, and then, with a final wave of their handkerchiefs, they entered a cab and were driven back to the city, where they proposed remaining with their friends for a visit, during their aunt's stay at Chestnut Villa.

As the good ship steamed swiftly down the harbor, the passengers began to leave the deck. Our young traveller looked around to see if he could discover any trace of the English lord, when he found that all the ladies had gone below. As he was preparing to follow their example, a young man approached him with the question:

"Going to Europe, hey?"

"Yes, I am thinking of taking a run across the Atlantic, and looking at some of the wonderful sights of Paris and other continental cities."

"Have an agency out that way, I presume?" said the stranger, raising his eye-glass.

"A son of the lord, I will bet anything," thought Thomas: "he carries an eye-glass, so he must be somebody. I will soon let him know that I am no agent.

"No, indeed!" he exclaimed, hastily; "I am travelling for pleasure; father seemed so anxious for me to make the grand tour, after I graduated, before I settled down to my profession. You know everybody that is anybody is expected to make that at the present day. We do not consider our education, finished any more than you Englishmen do, without first exploring the European Continent. The only difference with us is, that it costs so much more having the Atlantic to cross."

"In that case I should not think that the custom would be carried to any great extent, all Americans not being millionnaires."

"Of course poor people cannot afford it, but we of the wealthy class all do."

"You are a Nova Scotian, I presume, or a resident of one of the Upper Provinces."

"I am a Canadian, I am happy to say." (He will think I am a nobody if I call myself a Nova Scotian, thought Thomas).

"I have been taking a trip through Canada myself this year. I suppose it will soon be the correct thing for all Europeans of note to visit America, at least those who can stand the sea voyage. I should have liked very much to have seen the celebrated Annapolis Valley, where the beautiful apples are grown, but could not manage it. I am told it is a lovely spot. Ever been there?"

"Yes, I was born in that favoured locality."

"Indeed! I thought I understood you to say just now that you belonged in Canada."

"You do not seem to be very well posted in the geography of our country. Do you not know that all British possessions in America, except Newfoundland, are called Canada?"

"Are they? Pray, when were the Bermudas and the British West Indies annexed to the Dominion? They had a separate government when I left home. I should have thought that I would have heard something of the change, being in Canada all the while; but it must have taken place during my voyage out. How fast it is getting dark! It will soon be time to prepare for dinner. Have you ever been at sea before? Shall you be sea-sick?"

"No, I never made a very long voyage, but sufficient to test my nautical powers. We seem to have quite a number on board. I expect we shall have a very pleasant voyage, if we are only fortunate enough to have decent weather."

"Humph! that remains to be seen; I saw one group getting on board that would be sufficient to throw a wet blanket over any party, if they were inclined to be ever so lively. But let us take a trip below and look at them, that is, those who are not already doubled up in their berths. We are going to have a lively night outside."

"Am I not lucky," soliloquized Thomas, when he found himself alone in his state-room, "to think I should have been singled out from all the rest to be a companion for the lord's son, for of course he is the lord's son, he talks just like an aristocrat would. Ma always said I had such a distinguished air, that I was bound to attract attention in a crowd, and I think she was right.

"I saw a pretty girl on deck when we started, I hope she is a sister. I will ask him for an introduction to his folks to-morrow. Won't ma be pleased when I write to her? She won't be surprised, though. She always said I was a born diplomatist; but I guess even she hardly thought I should be hand and glove with the English swells before I was fairly out of Halifax harbor. I hope his pretty little sister will not be sea-sick to-night and spoil my pleasure for to-morrow. Ah! there is the dinner gong. I hope I will be lucky enough to get a seat by her side at the table; but I always am a lucky bird. What a clown I was not to tell him my name; how is he going to introduce me if he does not know my name? But perhaps the Captain will introduce us all, he can get our names from the office books. Well, I must go to dinner."

On reaching the dining-saloon, he found two long tables ready to receive the passengers; the Captain was seated at the head of one, while the first officer occupied the foot. Thomas was taken charge of by the chief engineer, and placed at the other table by the side of the stranger he had met on deck.

It was evident that the most important persons were at the other side of the saloon, and although a jolly lot were gathered around the engineer, Thomas felt that he had been ill-treated.

He glanced at the Captain's table and saw an ill-tempered old man, surrounded by his family, consisting of his wife and four grown children. Both the Captain and his officer seemed to have their hands full with the heads of the family, nor did their attempts to please them seem to be appreciated by their guests.

"Our Lord Arlingford and family," volunteered the stranger. "Ain't the young ladies handsome? Take a look,"—holding out his eye-glass to Thomas, —"cannot see one-half their charms with the naked eye, their brilliancy dazzles the common orb; veil and behold, but be careful of your heart, they are much too pure for ordinary mortals. They have been doing America, trying to capture a couple of rich heiresses for the young Honorables—have to repair the shattered fortunes of the house of Arlingford soon. Golden calves are getting rare in England, and so the necessity for exploring the territory of Uncle Sam. I wonder how they succeeded. Hope they selected husbands for the Hon. Misses Gladys and Constance as well. You see I have the whole crowd by heart. The one sitting at the left of the Captain is the heir of Arlingford Castle, its immense revenues, and a load of debts that have been breaking the backs of the owners for the past three generations. He is called the Honorable Frederick James. The other, the poet of the family, is known by the historical name of Cæsar Augustus. He published a volume once, but it did not add much to the family treasury. It was too sublime to be appreciated by the plebeians of England, consequently there was not much money in it. I expect our fashionable journals will have a glowing account of this American tour all written in his most poetical style."

"You are acquainted with Lord Arlingford and family?" now asked Thomas, his hopes rising again to the surface, for they had been gradually sinking since he made the discovery that his new friend was not a son of the Arlingfords. Still, he might be a lord, and could introduce him to the persons whose friendship he had been instructed to cultivate.

"Acquainted with them? No, indeed! As I told you before, they are much too pure for common clay. My father has a large iron foundry planted almost under the castle windows. Do you think they would for an instant tolerate a man who smelled of coal smoke? I am a tradesman's son; you, a resident of America, of course do not understand what that means in the eyes of an English aristocracy. Even our very gold is dimmed by the smoke of the furnace."

"You seem to have formed the idea, sir, that we know nothing about an aristocracy in Canada. I have much pleasure in correcting your mistake. We of the old families there have no more respect for those who soil their hands with trade than do the first class in England."

"Indeed! I presume your ancestors went over with Columbus, or was it some other man who discovered North America? I have it! You are a descendant of the Cabots; they were the British explorers, were they not? Please correct me if I am wrong, I am not very well versed in American history; but no, I must be mistaken there, for they were associated with trade. Perkins! Ah yes! I have it, now; you are a connection of the great Eli, of American fame. I have long been an admirer of his humorous writings."

"Yet you do not seem to be aware that the name Perkins with him is only a *nom de plume*, his true name being Melville D. Landon."

"Then he cannot claim the honor of being a relative of your distinguished family."

"No; as I have before informed you, we are Canadians; Mr. Landon is an American."

"Still you might trace your origin back to the same fountain-head, both Americans and Canadians being of European descent."

"No branch of our family, sir, ever settled in the United States. We can trace our lineage in a direct line to one of the most noble families of England, my Canadian ancestor being a younger son of a British Earl."

This was said in a loud tone for the benefit of the occupants of the Captain's table, and also to impress upon the stranger, the fact that he was talking to no ordinary person.

"Here is a snob of the first water," mentally quoted that individual. "He beats the English pattern. I wonder how the cash was made to fit him out for his tour, I will bet the old man's hands are not as white as his son's. He is too fond of telling what he is, to have been on the top round of the social ladder for any length of time. I hope we will have a short voyage; we certainly have a congenial lot on board.

"Well, to use a nautical term, I think I will turn in," he said aloud, as he arose from the table. "Good night all, and pleasant dreams."

"I trust that the last announcement will not destroy the gentleman's rest," remarked the engineer, "he seemed utterly crushed."

A general laugh went round the table, in the midst of which Thomas got up and walked away with a dignified air, without taking any notice of what he mentally called their rudeness.

CHAPTER VI.

Now, indeed, was Thomas in a dilemma. How to obtain an introduction to Lord Arlingford and family was the problem to be solved. Of course the first step on the ladder would be to cut the acquaintance of the stranger he had met when he first came on board. How unfortunate he had been after all, but it was a lesson not to be too ready to pick up with strangers because they happen to be well dressed and agreeable. After thinking for some time on the subject, he resolved to let things take their course for a few days, and perhaps in the meanwhile his infallible good luck would come to his aid. With this wise reflection he descended to his state-room, and in a short time he had forgotten his triumphs and defeats in a dreamless sleep, from which he was awakened by the ringing of the breakfast gong. Dressing himself quickly, he hastened to the dining saloon, where he found most of the passengers already assembled. The steamer was gliding along quite smoothly over the surface of the water, and everyone seemed to be in high spirits. Sea-sickness might be what the future had in store for them, but the present was for enjoyment. As our hero walked to the seat assigned to him the evening before, he glanced at the Captain's table, where he saw even the ill-tempered old lord had laid aside some of the gloom of the evening before, and was laughing in evident enjoyment of some joke from the table at the other side of the room.

As he seated himself he received a courteous good morning from his acquaintance of the previous evening, to which he responded rather stiffly. Looking up he met the eyes of the Honorable Miss Constance, and the smile with which she greeted his glance made his heart beat quickly, as he dropped his eyes upon his plate to conceal his exultation. He felt it would be no difficult matter to make the acquaintance of the Arlingfords if the ladies of the family noticed him without a formal introduction. He felt that he would find it hard work to play the agreeable to even the daughter of an English lord, with such a face, but the stake was too high not to make the most of it, and he knew it was his only chance to gain his point. Leaving the dining saloon he went on deck to smoke a cigar and mature his plans, quickly turning his back on his neighbour of the breakfast table as he saw him coming towards him. That gentleman needed nothing more to show him that his presence was not welcome, so he walked to the other side of the ship, where he soliloquized as follows:—

"The cut direct! Well, it is not the first time! I wonder how long it will be before he picks up the Arlingfords; that is what he is fishing for. Gad, there is one of the young honorables watching the performance. His fortune is made, now, if it can be called a fortune to make the acquaintance of that bankrupt gang. If he has plenty of the needful, it will not be very hard for him to gain the hand of one of the young ladies, especially if he can prove his descent from that earl he talked about, at dinner last night. The tarnish will be rubbed from his gold by shipping it across the Atlantic. I saw the Honorable Constance smile very sweetly on him at breakfast time; well, her face is certainly not her fortune, but her name may be.

"I guess the Honorable Cæsar is going to advance. He has been taking stock, giving old Brown's son the cut direct is a good trump in his hand. Exchange cigars, young gentlemen, and then for an introduction to the lady mother and the whole is completed; a grand triumph for them to carry him back to Arlingford castle to spend the Christmas holidays, as a trophy of the American tour. If they can only end the whole thing up with a wedding, they may get hold of enough to keep them afloat for a while longer. If something does not turn up soon there will not be a stone of the old castle left in the family by another year. I do not think the American tour was a success, if one may judge from their looks when they came on board. It takes gold to speculate out there as well as in England. A title, if it is not well gilded, is discounted even in America. Well, I hope the poor beggars will make out somehow, for I have no wish to turn them out of their musty old castle, and the pater will have it as sure as fate before another year, if they do not get a windfall in some way."

As our worthy traveller was thus communing with himself, the objects of his soliloquy had, as he already predicted, approached each other and exchanged cards, and even gone through the form of an introduction to Lady Arlingford, who had come on deck for her morning promenade. She received the young Nova Scotian with her most gracious smile, if the contortion into which she managed to twist her weazened face could be called a smile; but as young Brown had remarked, their fortunes were at a very low ebb, and Perkins appeared to be the only straw at which they could grasp,—so, frail as the support seemed, it was eagerly clutched. For the last few years they had staked their hopes on an American heiress, and when, after much planning, a sum of money had been gathered together to defray their expenses across the Atlantic, they had all set sail for that Western El Dorado, but on landing in the New World they had found that the average

American was as shy of the British pauper, even though he wrote Honorable before his name, as were the English. As their slender stock of money rapidly diminished they at length embarked for their native land, resolving to save what they could from the wreck of their home and settle in the western part of Canada, where they would meet with none who could know of their downfall.

At dinner the evening before, when they heard young Perkins declare so emphatically that he was not only wealthy, but also a descendant of an English earl as well, their fainting hopes were revived. Here was a young man with a fortune, going to Europe to enjoy it, and having the popular British contempt for everything American and Canadian, they immediately concluded that of course he had no influence to launch him on the sea of British society. Why not take him in hand, and if he could not be induced to wed one of the daughters of the house, and make liberal settlements, he might, out of sheer gratitude, take one or both of the sons back to America with him, and provide wealthy wives. At least the experiment was worth trying, and a little civility would cost nothing except pride. The way in which he had snubbed young Brown was conclusive proof that he was looking for higher game. Of course he would be an almost insufferable bore, but the Honorable Cæsar would tone him down by the time they reached England.

So, accordingly, the young people were called, a family council was held in the maternal state-room in the early morning, and it was decided to take him in hand at once.

The Honorable Cæsar was commissioned to make the first advances, and by luncheon time Mr. Thomas Perkins had gained the most supreme desire of his own and his mother's heart, he was hand and glove with members of the English aristocracy.

The stately old lord condescended to inform the Captain that he should like Mr. Perkins to have a seat at his table during the voyage. So, at luncheon, he was seated between the ladies Arlingford, where he would have the opportunity of choosing between the ladies, much to the amusement of his recent companions at the other side of the saloon; but this he treated with the lofty contempt which he considered it deserved.

Secure in his egotism, he could see nothing except jealousy in the rude jokes of the vulgar crowd. Being on a plane so far above the commonplace, he could afford to ignore all fun in which they were pleased to indulge at his expense.

Before the *Vancouver* reached Liverpool, he had got to such a degree of intimacy with the Arlingfords, as to accept an invitation from them to spend the Christmas holidays at their castle. When Lady Arlingford had given him the invitation, she had graciously added:

"I am afraid, my dear Mr. Perkins, that we cannot promise you very much in the way of amusement, as Lord Arlingford will require a long rest after his journey, his health being so poor; but if you can stand our quiet way of living, we will be so pleased to have you. The boys wanted to invite a few friends for Christmas, but the dear girls are so thoughtful for their father's comfort, that they decided against the proposal. Gladys suggested that we might ask you, as she heard you say that you loved a quiet country life, and her father endorsed her opinion. He almost looks upon you as one of the family. It was only yesterday that I heard him say that it seemed impossible it could only be one short week since we had met, you seemed like a person he had known for years. It is all the more remarkable, as he never cares to make the acquaintance of strangers."

"My dear Lady Arlingford, you and your charming family do me too much honor. I was indeed fortunate in meeting you. I was looking forward to a lonely voyage, and you have all been very kind. If you ever come to America again, you must be sure and make us a long visit. My father and mother will be so delighted to welcome you all at Chestnut Villa. Like yourselves, we reside most of the time in the country. I think you would like our home."

"I do not think that either Lord Arlingford or

myself will ever visit America again. We should never have mustered courage to cross the Atlantic this time, but the dear girls were so anxious to visit the new world, and their father never denies them anything on which they have set their hearts. I am afraid that the journey has been too much for him. He was ill most of the time after we landed, and we could not begin to do justice to your charming country. As soon as he was sufficiently recovered we sailed for home, and he will require a long rest when we reach there."

"Perhaps one or both of your sons might be induced to return to Nova Scotia with me," said Thomas, remembering his mother's injunction to secure a brace of husbands for Julia and Janie Maud, and resolving to strike while the iron was hot.

"Perhaps," replied her ladyship; "but there is time enough to think of that before your return. We will finish this journey before we plan another. You must make us a long visit, if we can interest you, before you go to Paris, and another before you sail for home in the spring."

"Many thanks for your kindness, my dear lady. I shall not fear dullness, for who could be dull in your charming presence? You will soon see home now. The man at the lookout reported land as you came on deck; it ought to be visible to us by this time. I am anxiously looking for the first glimpse of the home of my ancestors."

"Your ancestors were Irish, were they?"

"No, indeed, they were not! I have often heard my father say that my great-grandfather was the younger son of a British earl."

"I am not surprised to hear it, for you have the appearance of being well-born. Who was your ancestor?"

"I never heard his name, I will write and ask father. How stupid of me not to think of it before I left home! I might meet with relatives in England."

"I should advise you to do so, by all means. It is strange you do not know his name, as it is. You must be a peculiar people in America. I think I will go below, it is fearfully cold this morning. I do not wonder that the dear girls have not been on deck."

CHAPTER VII.

AFTER luncheon, the passengers, well wrapped in furs, went on deck to watch the ship enter Cork harbor. The Honorable Constance clung to Mr. Perkins' arm as if it already belonged to her. The way in which she asserted her claims to his attentions on every occasion was becoming decidedly irksome to him, but he endeavoured to smother his indignation, and make the best of the situation for the advantages it gave him to be tacked to the train of an English lord.

"She means to marry me," he said to himself. "I do not think they are very wealthy, and the girl is getting old, but she don't catch this bird with chaff. She thinks it will be a fine feather in her cap to capture such a good looking husband, but I want a better looking bride than she, even if she can write 'honorable' before her name. Besides, I do not believe she would suit the mater without a fortune. The dear old lady thinks that with my education and other advantages, I ought to secure a very fine prize in the matrimonial market, and I do not intend to disappoint her.

"They will probably be able to introduce me to a large circle of their friends, and they will be very exclusive, and if I manage right I will be able to take my pick—rich girls always take to something new.

"If I can take the heir to the title back to Nova Scotia with me, he will do for Jule. She is getting along, and I suppose the pater can put him in the way of increasing his capital. How the mater will delight to talk of my daughter, Lady Arlingford! Won't she pile on the airs though, when the event comes off!—that is, of course, if it does. But none of the ladies of the family for me, thank you! However, it will not do any harm for her to think she has me for the present."

"Why, Mr. Perkins! where are your thoughts flown? I have spoken to you twice, and could not make you hear. You are not very gallant I must confess."

"A thousand pardons, my dear young lady, I was dreaming of the ancient history of Ireland. The fact that this is my first visit to the old world must be my excuse for forgetting so delightful a companion. I promise not to offend again."

The smile and elaborate bow which accompanied this dose of flattery completely disarmed the young lady's anger, and as the ship was nearing shore she began to point out the various objects of interest to him, for a time really charming him.

He forgot that she owned one of the plainest faces in existence, in listening to the low, musical tones of her well-bred voice. She had read almost everything, travelled extensively, and was quite a brilliant conversationalist.

A few of the passengers went ashore at Queenstown, and their baggage was soon in the hands of the officials. The mail was sent ashore, the channel pilot came on board, and the *Vancouver* was headed for Liverpool.

The ladies retired to their cabin, and Mr. Perkins remained on deck to smoke, and dream of the future. What a brilliant picture his imagination called up as his fancy led him into the gay *salons* of London and Paris. He hoped, as the Arlingfords proposed leading such a quiet winter, that one, at least, of the young honorables, could be induced to accompany him to those gay capitals, where the golden portals would fly open at the magic name of Arlingford.

As he was thus dreaming away the twilight hours, a familiar voice sounded in his ears.

"Wa-al, I'll be darned, if it ain't Tom Perkins from Nova Scotia! How in the name of all rattlesnakes did you git away over here? But I'm rale glad to see you. And how's the old folks? Many's the piece of pumpkin pie your ma has give me for pickin' up chips and huntin' hen's nests for her when I was a little feller, and many's the time I've found enough eggs to fill her basket, and then carried them down to Larkins' store to swap for tea and sech like. How is the old girl looking? It's better than five year since I've seen her. I expect her hair is white by this time. But I'd have knowed you anywhere, you ain't a bit changed. Got a ship over in Liverpool?"

"I think you have made a mistake in the person. I have no recollection of ever meeting you before, and I am also happy to inform you that my mother never was under the necessity of exchanging eggs for tea."

"Mistaken! Wa-al, I guess not! I'd hev knowed you anywhere, you or any of the rest of old Bob Perkins' children. Your father was a right good one. I heard tell as how he made a lucky spec a short time after I left home the last time. Your ma was Julie Ann Smith—old Dan Smith, the rag pedlar's darter. I know the whole breed; but your ma was a mighty fine gal. Mistaken? Wa-al, I guess!

"No, Mr. gintleman, you don't come that off on me; but if you don't want to be civil, mum's the word. I'm sorry I intruded. I might hev knowed that you was too fine to be seen talking to an old salt, even if he was an old friend of the family. Times hev changed since Bill Howard was a boy. Then the Perkinses used to feel honored by an invitation to our house. Wa-al, sech is life. Good-morning, Mr. Perkins."

If anything could have added to the annoyance of Thomas, the sight of Mr. Brown, whom he had coolly ignored since the first day on board, sauntering leisurely up to the said Bill Howard, would have been sufficient. He was evidently a cabin passenger, or he would not be on that deck. If Brown got hold of him, and drew him out at dinner-time for the benefit of the Arlingfords, what in the world was he to do? He knew from experience that he might as well attempt to stop the wind from blowing, as try to stop old Bill's tongue when once he was started, and he also knew that Brown was just the one to start him. What evil genius had sent him on board of the *Vancouver*, when everything was working so smoothly? The fates had been against him from the very outset of his journey. He could not help shuddering even now, as he recalled the sudden appearance of the old aunt, the evening before his departure from home. He wondered if the spectre of the past was always to confront him at every turn, just as the golden apple was almost within his grasp.

"Well, the thing has got to be faced, and skulking won't mend matters, so I might as well go down to dinner," he concluded, with a sigh.

CHAPTER VIII.

He cast a furtive glance at the opposite table as he seated himself, and saw by the side of Brown, his old neighbor. Everybody seemed to be in high spirits, and—was it fancy, or had the engineer really heard Howard's version of his position in Nova Scotia? A scornful smile curled his lip as he met the eye of Perkins.

"You belong to Nova Scotia, Mr. Howard, I believe," he heard Mr. Brown saying, as he turned his head.

"Wa-al, yes," replied that worthy; "Nova Scotia is my native land, as the college men would say, and although I don't see much of it, I have a kind of a hankering for the old spot."

"I suppose everybody is rich out there; that the gold grows in the streets, and all you have to do is to stoop and gather it up,—in fact, that it is a sort of paradise where the younger sons of the English nobility go in order to make their fortunes, without soiling their hands with trade."

"English nobility, hey? I guess you won't find many English nobles stalking around there, loose. Every little while some snob of an Englishman comes along and tells the people that he belongs to the blue-bloods over here, when all the gals go wild over him for awhile, and take him around to picnics and parties, until his cash gives out, and then he ain't seen no more. A year generally finishes them, unless they get a fresh supply from home, and then they hang on a while longer. Anyhow, that's the way it used to be. I ain't been there for five years, now."

"But sometimes they go there to stay, do they not?"

"They always go there to stay, but they generally change their minds and move out when they have been there a spell."

"Don't one take root once in a while?"

"They may, but I never heard of one doing it in my time."

"I met a Mr. Perkins, a short time ago, who told me that he was the grandson of a British earl. He belonged down there. The fellow was rich; he was coming to Europe for a pleasure excursion."

"What! old Bob Perkins' son Tom? Wa-al, that *is* rich! Grandson to an earl, hey? Ha! ha! Why, old Bob used to be our hired man once. He married our hired girl, when I was a little feller; her name was Julie Ann Smith—old Dan Smith, the rag-pedlar's darter. But she was a nice girl, though, and made a mighty smart woman. There wasn't such a butter-maker in the country. She could always git a cent or two more a pound for her butter than anybody else, and law! the eggs that woman used to sell. I had a chance to know, for I used to be at her house half the time. She used to send me out to hunt the hen's nests, when she wanted the basket filled up to send down to the store; but they are rich now. Old Bob's got the biggest apple farm in the country; he has made a fortune from his apples alone, besides the potatoes and stock he sells. The two gals don't make butter, you just bet they don't! They have servants to wait on them, and drive out in their carriage with two big lamps on the sides, all dressed up in their silks and satins, with a man to look after the horses. Nobody ain't good enough for them to speak to now; but they say old Bob is the right sort yet, his money hasn't raised him a peg. He still goes around the farm in his old clothes, looking after his hogs and things, and don't go into their drawing-room, as they call it, from one month's end to another. An earl, hey? Wa-al, I do declare, that is the greatest I hev heard for some time. One has to travel to learn, they say, and I have certainly learned something by travelling to-day. That old Bob Perkins is the son of an earl, I guess will be a surprise-party for the folks to home."

"Indeed! You surprise me! But I still think you must be mistaken: the Mr. Perkins to whom I refer would not deign to soil his hands with work or trade."

"I don't know what you call trade, but if you refer to the Perkins that's on board of this ship at this blessed minute, why that's the very individual that I mean. That's certainly old Bob Perkins' son Tom; I would know him in Chiney. Many's the time I've toted him home from school on my sled, and I always got a piece of pumpkin pie or a doughnut from Julie Ann for bringing him. She was real good in them days; but, my sakes! ain't she stuck up now, though! But she never was above speaking to a feller, at the best of times."

"As you say that you have not seen him for five years, it is just possible that you may be mistaken, even now."

"Possible, but not probable, as a book would say. Tom's got a face like his mother's. Julie's face was about the size of a good big washtub, and looked like a cake of taller; besides, ain't his name Tom Perkins? You'd hardly meet with two Tom Perkinses that look like Julie Ann Smith. 'Tain't no use for the feller to say he ain't the one, for I know better.. I can't see the use, though, in him trying to make out 'tain't him; they are all fond of bragging, and I should think he'd want me to see him dressed up so fine. Who is he chumming with? They don't look like much potaters."

"The parties you refer to, are the Right Honorable Lord Arlingford and family, of Arlingford Castle."

"Oh, that's the way the wind blows, is it? The blue-bloods of England don't believe in work, I've heard. Wa-al, as I before remarked, times have changed since I was a boy. Who'd hev thought once that any of the Perkinses would be able to chum with lords; but they don't look like very rich folks, if they *are* lords."

A dead silence followed this dialogue, broken only by the clatter of the knives and forks.

Poor Thomas quickly swallowed his dinner, and, without daring to look at the Arlingfords, left the saloon. He went immediately to his state-room, where he threw himself, dressed, into his berth, and spent the entire night in trying to find some way out of his difficulty, but was no nearer a solution when the breakfast gong rang, than he had been on retiring.

He was surprised to receive a pleasant "good-morning," from each member of the Arlingford family. Miss Constance seemed even more determined than usual, to charm him. She was busily engaged during the entire meal, in planning excursions for his amusement when they reached Arlingford Castle.

"Come on deck, Mr. Perkins, and take your first look at dear Old England," she called, as she arose from the table. "What a pity that we should have passed Holyhead during the night! We shall land in a couple of hours, the Captain tells me, and then for home and the dear old castle. I wonder if all people love their home as well as we English do?"

"Be it ever so humble, there's no place like home, my dear young lady," said a voice at her elbow, and looking around she met the eyes of Bill Howard. He lifted his cap with a courteous "Good morning," which she answered by a glance of contempt, and her companion, with a look of bitter hatred, neither of which disconcerted the old sailor one whit.

Although Thomas felt pleased at his reception, after the revelation of the evening before, he could not help wondering why he was treated so cordially by those who appeared to scorn the very name of trade; but his vanity at last settled the question to his satisfaction, by deciding that his great personal attractions, coupled with his wealth, were irresistible. He felt so grateful to Constance for her condescension that he was on the point of proposing on the deck of the steamer, if fate, in the form of her sister, had not interrupted them.

"Come, Constance," said that young lady, "we had better go down and pack up. We will be in, in a short time, so let us have everything ready to leave the ship at once."

Could Thomas have been present, behind the scenes, at the family council held in Lady Arlingford's state-room, the evening before, he would not have gone below to prepare for his visit to Arlingford Castle with so light a heart.

The Honorables Frederick and Gladys were for cutting the insolent upstart without more ado, but the old Lord, still hoping to secure the American heiress, through the Perkins' influence, over-ruled this verdict, and was seconded by the Hon. Cæsar, whose vision of an unreceipted tailor's bill, which he knew he would have to raise the money to meet, almost as soon as he landed, inclined him to take a more lenient view of what they considered an offence. He hoped, by taking the part of Perkins, to be enabled to borrow the money of him to meet the bill. The Hon. Miss Constance, of course, was on the Perkins side.

"Who but a fool," she declared, "would hesitate an instant between a husband with plenty of money at his command, and teaching some upstart's brats for sixty or seventy pounds a year."

"Did not the sailor say," she replied, when her brother remonstrated, "that Tom's sisters had servants to wait upon them, and a carriage and coachman at their command? also, an unlimited number of silks?" When, she would like to ask, had she been able to indulge in a new silk? No, thank you! Gladys could become a model governess, if she had a fancy for that life, but for her part, she preferred a parvenu husband and a life of ease and luxury, even in the colonies. "If the gold is made of apples, it will be much sweeter than if it is tarnished with coal smoke; and what have we been living on for the past few years, if it is not old Brown's bounty? I am sure that he has never seen a cent of interest for the money that he invested in our estate."

So it was decided to overlook the exposure of the evening, and treat young Perkins the same as usual; only, as Gladys said, "It would not have been so bad if that odious Brown had not known all about it."

CHAPTER IX.

By the time that our travellers had gathered their baggage together, the *Vancouver* had dropped anchor in the Mersey, abreast of the Princess landing, and a small steamboat was alongside to take the passengers ashore. The Arlingfords had made no acquaintances on board except Mr. Perkins, so there was nothing to do but bid the Captain a polite good-by, and land. Their baggage was soon examined, when they drove direct to the depot, and in a short time were flying into the interior toward home.

Reaching London, they drove to a quiet hotel, stopping only long enough for luncheon, when they were again on the wing. They reached the end of their journey just as the sun was sinking into a bed of crimson clouds in the west, and enveloping the grand old castle in a flood of rosy light.

As they landed on the platform at Arlingburgh, a splendidly appointed carriage dashed up, which Thomas immediately concluded was sent to meet them; but a man sprang from the coach and grasped young Brown by the hand, giving him a most cordial welcome.

Just then an ancient-looking vehicle, drawn by two sedate old horses, and driven by a stately old coachman, who seemed to consider that part of the family dignity rested upon his shoulders, drew up by the side of the platform, and our travellers, after giving him a pleasant greeting, were promptly seated inside. The Hon. Frederick closed the door, raised his hat, and the carriage rolled away in the wake of the more showy equipage of the iron-founder.

They were soon driving through the gateway of the avenue leading to the old castle, where the great bell in the tower rang out a joyous peal to welcome the wanderers home. Chancing to glance at Gladys, Thomas was surprised to find her looking at him with a mixture of hatred and scorn, which she took no pains to conceal when she found that she was discovered.

As the carriage drew up at the grand entrance, the servants, who all appeared as ancient as the family and their surroundings, came forward to welcome them. The old lord gave his wife his arm to lead her up the steps, and Thomas followed his example, offering his to the young ladies; but Gladys drew back, scornfully, and passed quickly away, leaving her sister to accept his attentions. Entering the lofty hall, the rest warmly welcomed him to their home, and a servant was sent to show him to his room.

"One of the boys will come to show you the way to the dining-room. We will dine in half an hour," the old gentleman called after him, as he mounted the stairs.

Passing down a long corridor, where he saw the arms of the house of Arlingford engraved on every side, he was shown into a spacious chamber, where the servant left him. His toilet was quickly made, and he drew an easy chair to the cheerful fire that was burning on the hearth, and awaited the coming of the Hon. Cæsar, who he knew would be the one to guide him down stairs.

The dining-room was a grand old apartment, lighted by two lofty windows, and finished and furnished with black oak several centuries old. The magnificent silver, engraved with the armorial bearings of the house, seemed ample apology for the plainness of the food. Everything had a stately and old-world appearance, and the family harmonized well with their surroundings.

For the first time in his life Thomas felt abashed; he felt that he had no place among all this grandeur, and, try as he would, he could not recover his self-possession in the presence of the haughty Gladys. Although the rest of the family treated him with every kindness, he could not help feeling that by her he was looked upon as an intruder. He breathed more freely when the ladies had left the table and gone to the drawing-room; but he was not sorry when the hour for retiring arrived, and he could be alone in the room assigned to him. Even here the tall presses and massive bedstead, surrounded by rich, though faded, old tapestry, and lighted by two small wax candles, seemed oppressive.

The next day was Sunday, a day strictly observed by every member of the Arlingford household. After breakfast they all walked to Church, which was just outside of the park, and was, once, he was informed by Constance, with whom he walked, the private chapel of the Arlingfords. The building was of stone, and though fast sinking into decay, helped to tell of the former greatness of the family. The musty, high-backed pews and tall pulpit struck our hero with a feeling of awe, which was not lessened as the clergyman entered and began the service. The congregation, numbering about forty, all joined heartily in the service and in the singing, assisted by a dilapidated old organ as ancient as themselves. The service over, the family returned to the castle, with the air of persons who considered that they had done their duty, at whatever cost to their inclinations.

After luncheon, Thomas and Constance had a long walk together, when she entertained him with the history of the family since the Conquest. The evening was more dull, if possible, than the preceding one, and the hour for retiring an hour earlier.

CHAPTER X.

ON Monday a horse was procured with difficulty for Thomas, and the young people all went out hunting.

A riding costume had not figured among the requisites with which he had furnished his wardrobe, but looking out of the window before dressing, and seeing the Hon. Cæsar mounted for a canter in the park, it occurred to him that a different style of dress from that which was worn on ordinary occasions was necessary. He remembered reading in some novel a description of an Englishman arrayed for hunting, and he was positive that it mentioned, in particular, high-top boots and a quantity of bright colors. Going to his room after breakfast, he donned a base-ball costume, and an elaborately beaded smoking-cap. A pair of long rubber boots and tight-fitting tan gloves completed his outfit. The chill that came over him as he went into the corridor, warned him that he would need some warmer covering than the thin shirt in which he had been accustomed to play base-ball, so he returned to his room and pulled on a blue knitted jersey, and, thus equipped, he sallied forth, carrying in his hand a slight cane, which he intended to do duty as a whip.

When he reached the terrace, he found that they had all gone except Constance, who was loyally waiting for him. She was already mounted, and was in such a hurry to be off that she did not notice his dress, but calling him to follow, she broke into a sharp canter. He sprang into the saddle and gave his horse a slight tap with his cane, but he did not reach her side until they joined the rest of the party.

"Are we going to have a masquerade after the hunt to-day?" asked a young squire of Mr. Brown. "Some of our party seem to be of that opinion, and have dressed themselves this morning to save time."

"No; that, I presume, is the American style of riding-habit. The young gentleman is from the other side of the Atlantic."

"Who is he, Brown, anyway?" asked a third.

"A Mr. Perkins, of Nova Scotia, replied Brown; "and also a guest of the Arlingfords."

"Well, he is got up regardless, whoever he is. I must get Arlingford to introduce me. Where is he? I think I saw him ride up."

Just then the Hon. Frederick turned to look for his guest, and, horror of horrors! what in the world was the fellow rigged in? Everyone seemed to be highly amused with his appearance, and took no pains to conceal their merriment from the Arlingfords.

Frederick and Gladys cast a look of disgust at their sister, who stayed by his side, as if to shield him by her presence from the jokes of their neighbours. Although she was as much shocked as any at his appearance, she decided that his rig was what was worn in America when riding; and how was he to know, poor fellow, that it was going to make him ridiculous in England? She would tell him on their return, and the next time they went out, he could be arrayed as well as the best of them. Just then the signal was given for starting, and the two were for a time forgotten.

For about a mile they kept together, but a barrier appearing in the form of a low gate, Thomas deliberately pulled up, dismounted, and led his horse through, as his companion vaulted lightly over the rails.

"Come, hurry!" she cried, stopping and looking around to see if there were any witnesses to this performance; but they were well in the rear, so they took a fresh start and rode onward.

The excitement of the chase soon caused Constance to forget her companion, and when the next barrier was reached she was quite a distance ahead. This time he attempted to follow her example; he struck the horse with his cane and reined him straight for the fence. Clutching the animal around the neck as he raised from the ground, the soft rubber boots slipped from the stirrups, and he was flung upon his back in the mud, as the steed galloped away. Fortunately the ground was soft, and he was not hurt. He attempted to follow his horse, and soon found him quietly feeding. Remounting, he returned to the castle, wondering where the delights of hunting came in.

When the young people returned at night, they took no trouble to conceal the contempt they felt for him, and he almost fancied that even Constance was going over to the enemy.

The next morning a letter was found among the mail addressed to Lady Arlingford. With some surprise she opened it and read:—

"*My Dear Lady Arlingford:*

"It is with grief that I have to announce the death of your much respected cousin, Lady Alicia Vincent. A short time before her death, her only daughter married against her wishes, and at the time I was instructed to draw up a will in your favor, a copy of which I enclose. Trusting to hear from you at an early date, I remain,

"Yours faithfully,

"JOHN MATHEWS, Attorney."

A sigh of relief escaped from the poor tortured woman. She knew that her cousin was wealthy, and that they were saved without any further sacrifice. Looking over the will, she found that she was to receive about five hundred thousand pounds.

Thomas was overjoyed at hearing this, and in

the course of the day proposed to the Hon. Constance with high hopes; but he was wholly unprepared for the look of contempt which she gave him as she replied:

"The very idea of such a thing. Do you think that I, Viscount Arlingford's daughter, would condescend to wed a person of whom we know nothing, and an American also? I am surprised at your presumption!"

He announced his departure the following morning, much to the relief of the entire family, who were most anxious to be rid of him. The old family coach was brought around, and taking a final farewell of the Arlingfords, he was driven to the station, accompanied by the Hon. Cæsar. Before night he had taken up his abode in the Great Western Hotel in London, where he spent the entire evening in writing to his mother a glowing account of his visit to Arlingford Castle.

CHAPTER XI.

Any person unaccustomed to finding himself alone in a strange hotel can understand the feelings of Thomas the following morning. He began to think that after all he had not done wisely in so pointedly snubbing Mr. Brown. From what he had seen of that gentleman while visiting the Arlingfords, he was inclined to think that he occupied no mean position in the society of Arlingburgh. He had observed on the morning of that ill-fated hunting expedition, that he was about as popular as the young Arlingfords. Had he been contented with his acquaintance, he would, in all probability, have made it very pleasant for him during his stay in England, while his titled friends cruelly cut him as soon as they had obtained a glimpse of returning prosperity. Well, it was of no use crying over spilt milk; but what in the world was he to do with himself? Truly, there was not a great deal of fun in travelling in a strange country alone!

After considering the matter for some time, he

decided to hire a valet. "It will be a relief to have someone to talk to, if nothing more, he concluded."

The afternoon was spent in framing an advertisement to suit him, and after many fruitless attempts, the following was ready for the morning papers:—

"WANTED.—An American gentleman, travelling in Europe, wishes to obtain the services of a competent valet; a permanent situation to the proper person. Wages of no object. Best of references required. Apply to T. O. Perkins, Great Western Hotel, London."

On Friday he had certainly no need to complain of loneliness. He was kept busy during the entire day by attending to the applications for a situation. It appeared that an American gentleman, requiring a servant, was a person of some importance, even in London.

At last he found a person whom he thought would suit; a witty, good-natured Irishman, of about thirty years of age, with a face brimming over with fun and humor. Asking a few questions regarding wages, and settling this to his satisfaction, Thomas inquired for references.

"Lord Frederick Athol will give me a character, to be sure," replied the Irishman.

"Why did you leave the service of his Lordship?"

"Be me faith, and sure it was meself that he got too poor to kape any longer, poor boy!"

"Have you your character with you?"

"Be the holy powers, and do ye think that I

would travel around without me character, sure? And it's Mike Maloney that always carries his character with him, it is."

"Let me see it, please."

"See me character! And it's surely crazy the man is, to want to see me character! He will be after wanting to look at me sowl next."

"I wish to look at the written proof that you are really what you represent yourself to be. How am I to know that you are not an escaped convict, if I am not furnished with proof to the contrary?"

"Howly Moses! Didn't I tell ye that Lord Frederick Athol would be my riference? You want no better proof than his word, for a nobler gintleman than himself niver lived, God bless him!"

"That may be; but, in the meanwhile, where am I to find this same Lord Frederick? You do not carry him in your pocket, do you?"

"You will find him just a few blocks away. It's poor lodgings for the loikes of himself; but times hev changed, poor lad, since the days when the Athols lived in the old castle down in dear old Tipperary, where there was plinty and to spare, and niver a sowl to want for a bite nor a sup. Jist stip into a cab, and it'll whisk you down to the poor lad's lodgings in less than no time, sure."

"Very well. Step into the next room and bring me my hat and overcoat, and you might as well come with me, for I do not know the way."

The coat and hat were quickly brought, and the two started. Mike kept his master amused during the journey with his droll remarks, and he began to congratulate himself on getting hold of a treasure.

Arriving at his Lordship's lodgings, he was ushered up a steep flight of steps, at the top of which his guide knocked upon a door, which was immediately opened by a young man, whom Mike addressed as "me lord."

"And it's Mr. Perkins, from America, that I have brought to see yoursilf, me lord."

"I am very much surprised at you, Michael, for daring to take such a liberty," answered his Lordship.

"I humbly beg your pardon for this intrusion," now said Thomas; "but as I engaged this fellow for a servant, and he referred me to you for his character, I was obliged to bring him with me for a guide, as I am a stranger in London."

"I thought I gave him a written character when he left my employment."

"Sure and ye did, too, but it would puzzle mesilf to tell where it has gone, now; but tell the gintleman that I airns me wages fully, does me dooty faithfully, and niver makes mistakes at all, at all."

"I have always found you to be a very industrious, sober young man, and always ready to attend to your duties, and it was from no fault of your own that I was obliged to dismiss you. Mr. —ah—Perkins, I can fully recommend him as a valuable servant; he has been in my employ for years, and I always found him at his post, and now, as my time is limited, I will bid you good-afternoon."

Thomas would have liked much to remain longer and converse with his Lordship, but the door was held open politely for him to depart, so there was nothing for him to do except go.

"Confound his insolence," he muttered; "I feel like agreeing with Brown, after all. You never can get on friendly terms with those old aristocrats, they think they belong on a higher plane than ordinary mortals. Well, I have a guide now, and will take in the general sights of London, if I cannot get among the upper ten. I wonder what the poor old mater would say, if she knew that her favorite son had to fall back on an Irish servant for a companion."

After dinner, Mr. Perkins, accompanied by Mike, started for the theatre. He secured a box at the office of the "Great Western Hotel," and dressed in faultless evening costume and immaculate white kids, he sauntered leisurely to his box, followed by Mike, carrying his hat, coat and cane. A superb bouquet adorned the lapel of his perfectly-fitting coat, and he flattered himself that he made a striking picture. He had obtained an eye-glass for the occasion, and as soon as he was seated, he began a survey of the audience. Mike, who had never been at the theatre before, was for a time entranced by the splendor around him; but the natural loquacity of the Irishman soon got the upper hand of his surprise.

As Mr. Perkins imagined, they made a striking picture, and glasses from all parts of the house were turned upon their box. It was evidently not a common occurrence in London for a gentleman to take his servant to the theatre with him for a companion.

A pompous old dowager occupied the nearest box, accompanied by two handsome young damsels. Mike attracted considerable of their attention, and as he perceived their amusement, he arose, pulled his forelock, and bade them a polite good-evening.

"Sit down, you scoundrel!" commanded his master, "and do not let me hear another word out of you this evening."

"Begorra! sure and it's not mesilf that kin howld me tongue for the intire night. Shure, this must be the gateway to Heaven, that his holiness the priest talks about. It's beautiful, it is!"

"Will you hold your tongue?"

"Faith, and it's mesilf that will try to, if it displases your honor for me to talk."

"Have we something new in the way of entertainment this evening?" said a voice behind them. "I never heard of turning the boxes into a portion of the stage; but there is always something new in the wind, and a couple of actors have certainly lost their bearings to-night. It is decidedly original, if nothing more."

Mr. Perkins turned and gave the speaker a scornful glance. But Mike was not going to be contented with this. He sprang to his feet, and, with blazing eyes, began:

"Begorra, you blackguards, how dare you say such things about my master, Mr. Perkins from Nova Scotia? He is no more an actor than yourself! He is one of the famous apple-growers of America. Sure, it was mesilf that helped him pick apples last year as big as the whales of an Irish jaunting car. You niver seen sich apples in England."

"No! we never see any American fruit here."

"Oh, well! we sind you over the pickings sometimes; but, of course, we kapes the best for home consumption, as it were."

"Mike, you villain, if you do not keep still you shall leave the building," said his master.

Just then the rising of the curtain claimed all Mike's attention, and for some time his master had no further trouble with him; but when the heroine of the piece called in heart-rending accents for someone to save her from the villain who was persecuting her, Mike's chivalry was instantly aroused, and crying, "Yes, me' poor darlint, I'll help you!" he sprang over the railing of the box, which was in the front tier, and dropping upon the stage, he bore off the poor darlint, despite her struggles. He carried her straight to his master's box before he was interrupted. The curtain was lowered, and the actress slipped away amid the shouting of the audience.

Poor Thomas, thoroughly crestfallen, prepared to leave the building, before any further mishaps could befall him; but, just as he reached the grand entrance, a dapper little dandy accosted Mike with the question:

"Where do you live?"

"With my master, Mr. Perkins, at the Grand Western Hotel," answered Mike, proudly, before Thomas could prevent him.

Once outside, Thomas hailed a cab, and was soon in his private room at the hotel. Here he ordered Mike to leave him, and drawing a chair to the fire, tried to think what he had better do next. For about an hour he meditated, and at last concluded to pack up and return home by way of New York. Truly, he had had enough of Europe. He would now finish his tour in America, among civilized beings.

When he had reached this conclusion, the door was suddenly opened, and a waiter announced Sir Rupert Mordaunt. Thomas looked up, surprised at the intrusion, and perceived the same dandy who had inquired of Mike for his address as they left the theatre.

Sir Rupert advanced and smilingly held out his hand, with the remark:

"Mr. Perkins, I believe."

"Yes, my name is Perkins," replied our hero, wondering what mischief Mike had been up to now.

"Excuse me, Mr. Perkins, for the liberty of calling, but I was so amused at the antics of that servant of yours, that I was most anxious to make the acquaintance of his master. Where in the world did you pick him up? He is certainly quite an original character; but he, surely, is not an American."

"No: I engaged him in London a few days ago. My servant was obliged to return to America, and I had to replace him with what I could get hold of. He had served in the employ of Lord Frederick Athol, an Irish peer, for several years, and he gave him a good character, but I am finding him almost insupportable."

"Pardon me for the suggestion, but is it not a little out of the common rule for a gentleman to take his servant to the theatre with him as a companion? Our English servants are not accustomed to such treatment."

"It may be; but, being a stranger in London, and finding the time hanging rather heavy on my hands, I started out, taking Mike with me as a guide, as he professed to know all about the city.

I came up from the country a few days ago, where I had been visiting some friends—a Lord Arlingford and family—whom I met in America. In fact, we came over together, and I was to spend Christmas with them; but a death in the family caused a change of plans, and I came away. I am waiting here for a few days for letters from America before crossing to Paris, where I propose to spend the winter."

"In the meanwhile, you find a London hotel rather quiet after the gaiety of Arlingford castle. I was there once, you see, and I know all about it. Did not your friends, the Arlingfords, provide you with letters of introduction to their London acquaintances?"

"No; I suppose they were so overwhelmed with grief that it escaped their memory."

"Probably. I can imagine their grief to be almost overwhelming, especially as the lady's death put them in possession of somewhere near half a million. But I am forgetting my errand. My dear Mr. Perkins, Mademoiselle La Moin is so very much annoyed by the rough treatment of your servant, that she thinks you owe her an apology, and I am sent to ask you to join us at a little supper, where you will meet the—ah—charming Mademoiselle, and have the opportunity of presenting your apologies in person."

I shall certainly be most happy to apologize to

the lady for the awkward blunder of my servant. When does the supper take place?"

"This evening, at once. Will you come with me?"

"With the greatest of pleasure. I will be ready as soon as I call Mike."

"Why, you cannot take him with you. I know London, and can guide you quite as well as he."

"I can assure you that I have no intention of taking him with me. For the future I will dispense with his services as a guide. I only wish to request him to remain up for me, it is so disagreeable having to put away your own c.othes."

"Of course it is; but you have a jewel of a servant, if you can manage to keep him awake until the wee sma' hours. I never could get one to do it."

"Mike will, I assure you."

Mr. Perkins answered as confidently as if he had known Mike for years, instead of hours, and was quite accustomed to having him put away his clothes for him every night.

CHAPTER XII.

Sir Rupert's carriage was waiting at the door, and in a short time Thomas found himself the centre of a gay group, consisting of some half dozen fast young ladies and a number of equally fast young gentlemen.

There was a fair sprinkling of titles among them, and again his star seemed to be in the ascendant.

After all, the blundering Irishman had given him a powerful lift on the social ladder. He might have remained in London many years and not had as much notice taken of him as Mike had procured for him in one evening.

Mademoiselle La Moin accepted his apologies graciously, and everyone seemed to be in high spirits.

When he bade his hostess good-night, she gave him a cordial invitation to call frequently during his stay in London. "But do not bring Mike with you," she added, with a shudder. "I do not feel inclined to renew the acquaintance. I can hear him yet telling me not to be afraid, that his master, Mr. Perkins, would protect me and take me back to America with him. America is apparently but once removed from Paradise in his estimation."

"It certainly was a portion of the programme that the audience was not expecting, although it would be a difficult matter to make some of them believe it," said a gay young lordling, joining the group. "Mr. Perkins, I should advise you to take the fellow out with you frequently, he would soon make you one of the most popular men of London."

"I do not think that I should care for popularity obtained in that way," replied Thomas, and, with his most graceful bow, he withdrew.

Sir Rupert drove him back to his hotel, and then went to join his boon companions at their club, where they had all agreed to meet to discuss what they called their new curiosity.

"Who is he, Mordaunt?" asked one of the party, as they all flocked around Sir Rupert on his return. "Is he worth taking up?"

"I do not know; but, from what I have been able to gather, I should say, yes. The Arlingfords picked him up in America, and brought him over with them. They were out there, you know, trying to find someone to save the estate, which was just about gone. He must have had quite a pocketful of the ready, or they would not have been bothered with him.

"They had scarcely got their feet on English soil before a cousin snuffed out and left them a fortune, so Mr. Perkins, being of no further use to them, promptly received his dismissal from Arlingford Castle, and comes up to London for a time, to look for new adventures. The Arlingfords, being in such deep grief for the dear departed, forgot to give him a letter of introduction to their friends, so he is left at the mercy of his servant, who acts as guide. Fancy an Irish servant guiding his master to the dress circles of the most popular theatre in London! Just like the national cheek! But what an item for one of the fashionable journals! Well, whatever his standing in America, he is an out-and-out cad. I would like to have him meet the Arlingfords in London, but I do not suppose they will be up for some time. They will have to go into seclusion for the dear departed."

"Who in the world are the Arlingfords?" now interrupted one of the group.

"Oh! some of Sir Rupert's swell friends in his palmy days, I expect," answered another.

Sir Rupert laughed good-naturedly as he replied:

"Yes, I spent a fortnight once at Arlingford Castle with the governor. Old Lady Arlingford was the old boy's young love, but she jilted him for Viscount Arlingford's title, and the old fellow took it to heart. He wanted to make matters all right by marrying his beloved nephew to the Honorable

Gladys, one of the most hideous females it was ever my fate to behold. My refusal, coupled with a few other misdemeanors, cost me a fortune, and left me a titled beggar.

"Well, we will turn Perkins over to Evelyn. If he and Mademoiselle La Moin cannot make something out of him, I give him up as a hopeless case. Evelyn, you owe me my revenge to-night; to-morrow I will have to run down into the country and see the mater, if I want to be left alone to spend my Christmas in peace. So let us get to work, for it grows late."

They were soon all seated at the card table, and Mr. Perkins was for a time forgotten.

CHAPTER XIII.

When Thomas reached his room, he found the jewel of a servant curled up on the hearth-rug, fast asleep. After several vain attempts to awaken him, he gave up the undertaking and went to bed, leaving him there; and, for a man with a servant, he managed to do without his services very well. He was soon fast asleep, and was again, in his dreams, mingling with the gay crowd in which he had spent the evening.

The next morning he received a visit from Lord Evelyn, one of the guests at Mademoiselle's little supper the evening before.

Thomas ordered luncheon in his private room, where they were waited upon by Mike. They spent the afternoon in driving around London in Lord Evelyn's private carriage, and although highly elated with his present position, experience had warned Thomas to be prepared for failures.

He glanced furtively around every corner, almost expecting to see some Nemesis suddenly arise and denounce him as an impostor; but the afternoon wore away, and nothing happened to mar his enjoyment.

They dined at his lordship's club, with a small, though select circle, and afterwards adjourned to the billiard-room, where his new friends readily undertook to instruct him in the game.

The anxiety with which all seemed so ready to serve him, might have aroused the suspicions of a less observing person than Thomas, but his egotism set it all down to the fact that he was a person of no common appearance, and even when he arose from the card table late in the evening, the poorer in purse by some fifty pounds, he still felt that his new friends had no intention of dealing otherwise than fairly with him.

On his return to the hotel, he found a daintily-tinted little note from Mademoiselle La Moin, inviting him to a quiet little dinner the following evening.

"Just a few very intimate friends," she wrote, "and we shall be so disappointed if you do not honor us with your presence. We will have music, and spend as quiet an evening as if we all attended divine service."

Late as was the hour, Thomas called Mike, who, for a wonder, was waiting for his return, to bring his writing desk, and a note of acceptance was carefully written and delivered to him, with the injunction to have it sent the first thing in the morning. His new friends had said nothing to him about attending church, but he concluded to select one at hap-hazard.

After breakfast the following morning, he arrayed himself for the street, and sauntered out alone. He walked boldly into the door of the first building he came to bearing a resemblance to a church. There were but few persons inside as he entered, but he decided that it was owing to the fact that he was too early. He seated himself about half-way up the centre aisle, and began to look around. After waiting for some time, and finding that the congregation did not increase, he ventured to ask someone near when the service would begin.

"What service?" inquired his listener.

"Why, the service in this church, to be sure."

Instead of answering this question, the person addressed uttered a piercing scream and fled.

"What in the world is the matter, now?" thought Mr. Perkins.

He was not left long in doubt, for a policeman soon appeared and promptly took him in charge. In spite of his resistance, a pair of handcuffs were quickly snapped upon his wrists, and he was hustled into a waiting cab at the door and driven to a police-station.

When they reached that building, he was placed

in charge of another official, who led him through a long corridor and down a flight of stone steps, at the bottom of which his guide paused and opened a door. He was pushed into a room without ceremony, and the door quickly closed and bolted.

Looking around, he saw the light entered from a grated window high in the wall. The furniture consisted of an iron bedstead, on which was a hard mattress and a pair of coarse blankets, a rough deal table, and a couple of straight-backed wooden chairs.

For some time he sat, stupefied by the suddenness of his capture, but at last concluded that he had been kidnapped by some band of outlaws, for the purpose of robbery. He had often read of such things, but had never known that they were bold enough, at the present day, to walk into so public a building as a church, in broad daylight, and carry off a man to gain a reward.

"They won't find much to rob me of, if I can help it," he said to himself, as he emptied his purse of all the paper it contained, and taking off his shoes and stockings, he smoothed out the bank-notes and placed part in the bottom of each stocking, which he then drew on again. He next transferred all the gold, amounting to ten sovereigns, to a letter, and placed it in an inside pocket. After he had thus secured the greater part of his wealth, he dropped his purse, which now only contained a few pieces of silver, carelessly into his pocket again, concluding it would have to go along with his watch and ring.

For about an hour after this he was left undisturbed; but at last he heard a step coming down the stairs, and he made up his mind to submit quietly to the robbery that he felt certain would now take place, if by that means he could only regain his freedom.

But his jailer came into the room bearing a plate of coarse bread and a pitcher of water, which he placed on the table, and withdrew without saying a word. Mr. Perkins sprang to the door as he was leaving, and asked him where he was and what he was brought here for; but the only reply he received was, "Don't know," as the door was quickly locked in his face.

He paced the room for the next hour like a caged lion, and, at last, thoroughly exhausted, threw himself upon the hard bed and dropped asleep. He was awakened by the noise of a key turning in the lock, and his jailer entered with his supper, consisting this time of hard bread and a bowl of weak tea. He placed a smoky lamp upon the table, took the untouched dishes brought at dinner-time, and was leaving the apartment; but his prisoner had been too quick for him, and was already in the door.

An alarm was quickly sounded, and as Thomas rushed up the stairs, he was promptly seized at the top and walked down into his cell again, and the door barred in his face before he had time to recover his breath.

"Well, I may as well be poisoned as starved to death, for it is quite apparent that I won't get away from here to-night, and I may need all my strength to get away at all. So I suppose I had better try and eat some of this trash," he said, contemptuously, taking up a piece of the bread.

He consulted his watch before he began, and found that it was about the hour that he would be expected at Mademoiselle La Moin's quiet little dinner-party. He wondered what she would think if he did not keep his appointment, after accepting her invitation.

The food, though coarse, was welcome, and he finished it all before he left the table.

He spent the evening in walking around his cell, and at last lay down and watched the window for the first streak of dawn; but how slowly the hours passed. His lamp had long gone out, and he had no means of knowing the time; but he at last decided that the London fogs, of which he had read, were really obscuring the light of the sun, for certainly twenty-four hours had passed since the jailer had brought him his supper. At last tired nature asserted herself, and he fell into a troubled sleep.

When he awoke it was broad day, and looking at his watch, he found it was nearly eight. A short time after, his breakfast was brought in, and he managed to find out from his jailer that he had spent the last twenty-two hours in one of the cells of the police-station; but what he had done to deserve such treatment, was more than he was able to discover.

About ten the man again made his appearance, and commanded him to follow. He was led into the court-rooms and placed among a disreputable looking crowd before the judge. After several cases had been disposed of, his Honor told him to stand up.

"Your name and residence?" inquired his worship.

"Thomas O. Perkins, of Nova Scotia."

"You are charged, sir, with being an escaped lunatic, who entered a music hall on Sunday morning, and nearly frightened a poor unprotected female into fits with your violence. What have you to say in your defence?"

"After breakfast I went out for a walk, and entered what I supposed to be a church. As the congregation increased very slowly, I asked a lady sitting near me at what hour the service would begin; but, instead of answering, she screamed and fled as if a thousand fiends were after her. Soon a stranger put in an appearance, placed handcuffs upon my wrists, and brought me here, where I have been unlawfully detained."

"You have been detained, but not unlawfully;

and, as your prosecutor has not appeared, you may go, you are free."

"And how, sir, am I to be recompensed for the wrong that I have sustained at your hands?"

"You have met with no wrong at our hands. We only do our duty when we detain those who are brought to us."

"Were I in America, I could have you prosecuted for false imprisonment."

"You are not in America, but in London, and you had better leave here before I give you in charge for contempt of court. I have already shown you too much lenity."

On hearing this threat, Mr. Perkins concluded that discretion was the better part of valor, and quickly made his escape into the street. He hailed a cab, and was soon at his hotel. He summoned Mike, and ordered his breakfast brought to his room, where he made a hearty meal. He inquired if he had had any callers in his absence, and was answered in the negative. He wondered if it was too early to call on Mademoiselle La Moin, but decided it would be better for him to wait until after luncheon. He sent Mike for the morning papers, and was soon occupied in reading the police report, where he found his own name disagreeably prominent; but he hoped that it would escape the eyes of his friends, and decided to say nothing about the matter.

CHAPTER XIV.

A few moments after Thomas decided to say nothing about his arrest, Lord Evelyn was announced, and as he arose to meet him, he was greeted by a boisterous laugh from that gentleman.

"Well, Perkins, what in the world have you been up to? Drunk and disorderly on the London streets? I see by the morning papers that you spent the night at the police-station. Don't you think it is rather a depraved taste that would prefer such a place to being present at one of Mademoiselle's charming little dinners? But I forget that you have never yet attended one. She is furiously angry at you for treating her invitation in such a shabby manner. The little lady is accustomed to have her every whim obeyed, so you had better make your peace with her without any delay."

"Must I explain why I was detained? She might not know."

"You need not flatter yourself that she will not

know. You will have to stand any amount of chaff on that score. How in the world did it happen? One of Mike's pleasant little comedies, of course. I am afraid that you will have to discharge him, if you do not want your social reputation ruined."

"No, Mike is clear of this scrape. I went for a walk in the morning, and, happening to be near a church, I resolved to drop in and pass away an hour. I asked a woman sitting near at what time the service would begin; but, instead of answering, she cleared out and gave me in charge. The first thing I knew, I was locked up, without a chance to say a word in my own defence. I have heard of countries where they arrest people for not attending divine service, but I never knew before that they locked them up for going there in England. But I suppose that I got into some big bug's private chapel."

"It would have been better for you, in this case, to have taken Mike for a guide. I can fancy him standing qu...tly and letting them put the bracelets upon his wrists. If he did get you into a scrape when he went with you, you must allow that it was a lucky one for you; for, by his performance, you obtained an introduction to one of the most charming young ladies in London."

"If I was in America, I could make them smart for doing such a thing."

"You could obtain satisfaction here, but I should

not advise you to try. It would not be pleasant to have a trial over it. You seem to be very comfortable here, but you would find it much more pleasant if you were to take private lodgings. You intend to remain some time in London, do you not? You can receive your friends much more conveniently in lodgings."

"I was thinking of going to Paris soon."

"If I were in your place, I would spend part of the winter in London. You are just beginning to get acquainted here, and we can make it quite pleasant for you after a time. You will have the same ground to go over again in France, only it will be more difficult for you there, owing to the fact that you will have hard work to converse with the Parisians."

"I am considered a capital French scholar."

"You may be in America, but you will find it will not work to a charm in Paris.

"I can help Mike look after you. I won't agree to have anything to do with your church-going, for I am not much of a hand at that sort of thing; but in any other amusement you will find me there. Now, if you will call that son of Erin with some refreshments, I will help you partake, and then we will go and make your peace with Mademoiselle the first thing. After that we can have a look around for lodgings. I think I know of some that will just suit you. A friend of mine went out of town for the winter last week, and I do not think his rooms are re-let yet. They are in a nice, quiet quarter, and only just a short distance from everywhere."

Mike soon had a tempting little lunch on the table, which our two friends fully appreciated. Then, equipping themselves in their outdoor garments, they sallied forth. They hailed a cab, and were soon in the pretty little drawing-room of Mademoiselle, awaiting the appearance of their fair hostess. She did not keep them waiting long, however, but tripped in almost as soon as they were announced, and swept his lordship a graceful courtesy, scarcely deigning to notice his companion.

"You see, I have brought you a martyr this afternoon, my dear young lady. Do not prolong his sufferings by your coldness, for he has already gone through enough to plunge an ordinary mortal into the lowest depths of despair, without our charming Mademoiselle withdrawing the light of her countenance from the poor boy."

Thomas gave his lordship a grateful glance for the effectual way in which he had pleaded his cause; but he did not feel as well pleased as his friend continued, explaining the story in his own way, and preventing him from making what he considered would be a suitable apology for his absence the previous evening. He could not tell, from the way in which his lordship told his tale, whether he was trying to gain the sympathy of the lady for his unfortunate friend, or was only trying to make him appear ridiculous in her eyes.

"You see, my dear young lady," Evelyn continued, "one of the most unfortunate young men on this side of the Atlantic. Going out, like the dutiful son that he is, to obey the instructions of his loving mother, who, of course, admonished him before leaving home not to neglect the holy Sabbath, but attend on the ordinances of divine worship in the order in which they occur, he was seized upon yesterday morning by some fanatic of a woman and given in charge of a policeman, who locked him up as an escaped lunatic. Faith! and I do not wonder that he was considered a fit subject for a madhouse, wasting his time wandering around the city churches on a day like yesterday; but you must not be too hard on the poor boy for not keeping his appointment, for how could he, when a number of iron bars were between him and liberty? You should consider it punishment enough to be kept away from your charming self, and fed upon bread and water in the cold seclusion of an empty cell, without anything further. So, my darling Katie, just put your little hand in his, and tell him that you are glad to see him, after all he has gone through; and, also, that you will be so pleased to have him dine with you this evening in the company of his most intimate friend, the Right Honorable Lord Evelyn."

"Not at all, my lord! I have an engagement

this evening; so you can just take yourself out of my way. I shall be pleased to have Mr. Perkins dine with me to-morrow evening, and escort me to the theatre afterwards. That is, if it is not against his principles to go to the theatre on Christmas Eve. Perhaps he prefers attending church. You can come, too, if you like. And now, gentlemen, I will have to say good-afternoon; a poor actress's time is not at her own disposal. I shall expect you early to-morrow evening, Mr. Perkins; I dine at seven sharp."

"I shall be most happy to be on hand," answered our hero, as he withdrew, with what he considered a most killing bow.

"Mademoiselle La Moin will expect us, but she will also expect a small tribute in the way of diamonds for a Christmas gift," remarked his lordship when they reached the street.

"She won't get anything very valuable from me: but she will never forgive us if we fail to remember her, so we might as well go to a jeweller's and select our gifts now, and have it over."

They were soon looking over a glittering pile of jewelry, from which his lordship selected a handsome locket, set with small, though fine, diamonds, for which he paid the sum of fifty pounds.

Thomas was considerably startled at hearing this; but, not to be outdone in generosity, he purchased a bracelet set with pearls and rubies, for which he paid the sum of sixty pounds. This, with the fifty he had lost at cards a few evenings before, made the thousand dollars that he had been given to cover the expenses of his tour, considerably smaller. But, remembering his mother's advice to spend his money royally when in the society of distinguished persons, he handed it over with a smiling face.

From the jeweller's they went to the lodgings that his friend had spoken of, and found them still untenanted; so Thomas engaged them, and returned to the hotel to pack up and take possession at once, in order to get settled before Christmas.

Mike soon had everything ready for their departure, and before night they were comfortably settled in their new abode.

CHAPTER XV.

After Mike had arranged everything to his own and his master's satisfaction, he asked permission to spend the evening with some friends.

"Why, Mike!" replied his master, "I was not aware that you had friends in London. I thought you hailed from the Emerald Isle!"

"Bedad, and so I do, sure. But do you think that a gintleman like me Lord Athol spent all his time at home like some common farmer? No, indade, he did not! He travelled all over the world, as it were, and took me along with him as a companion, your honor."

"His lordship had you for a companion, did he?"

"Well, not exactly; but, as he was young, poor boy, I had to sort of look after him, you see, and kape a fatherly eye on him. I wonder what he is doing to-night, poor lad! and a sorry Christmas he'll spend all alone by himself, and no one belonging to the old castle about him at all, at all!"

"Is it to see him that you wish to go out to-night?"

"See him! Do you suppose I would take such a liberty? No indade! it's to see me own blessed cousin, swate Nora O'Connor, from Tipperary. She is lady's maid to Lady O'Mullin. That's where I want to go."

"Well, you can go; but I want you to return early, as I shall not go out this evening."

"And it's meself that will be in by tin, by the clock, without fail. Will your honor be after wanting anything before I lave?"

"No; you can go now."

For some time after his servant's departure, Thomas sat gazing into the fire and dreaming of the future, where Mademoiselle La Moin's bewitching face played a prominent part. With what a charming smile she had set aside his lordship that afternoon. How plainly she had showed that he, Thomas, was her favorite. He wondered if his mother would consider the actress good enough for her daughter. If not, would he dare defy her? He drew the bracelet he had purchased that afternoon from his pocket, and gazed at it, wondering if she would be the recipient of many such gifts. If she had many such friends as his lordship, the contents of her jewel-case would be quite a fortune for her. Yes! he would win her from all his titled friends, and carry her back to Chestnut Villa with him.

Poor, misguided youth! Will not even a single doubt enter to mar the glowing picture? How long would the lively little French actress be contented to remain in the quiet seclusion of Chestnut Villa, even could she be induced to go there?

The tiny clock on the mantle striking ten, aroused him from his reverie. "I will have no callers after this hour," he thought, "so I might as well go to bed. I wonder where that scoundrel of a Mike is! He promised to be back before ten; but I suppose he has not seen his cousin for some time, and the hours are going more swiftly than he is aware of. Well, I do not need him very much now; but he must not be given too much liberty, or he will become unmanageable. I will go to bed and try to get some sleep, for it is precious little I will get to-morrow night."

The following day seemed to crawl, so slowly did the time go; but at last the hour for dressing arrived, and Mike's duties were fairly begun. His hair was most elaborately curled, and the few stray hairs that adorned his upper lip, and which he dignified by the name of moustache, were carefully waxed.

He had spent nearly an hour over the selection of his button-hole bouquet, at the nearest florist's, and nearly another had been whiled away before he could decide on the exact tint of his gloves. But at last everything was arranged to his entire satisfaction and taking a last, lingering look at his reflection in the glass, he set forth for the home of Mademoiselle.

Early as he thought he was, he found Lord Evelyn and several more young gentlemen before him. A small stand had been placed near the entrance for the reception of the little lady's Christmas gifts, among which he soon discovered Lord Evelyn's diamond locket. He was in doubt if he should place the bracelet among them or deliver it to his hostess, but at last he walked boldly to the spot where she was standing, and presented it with a killing bow.

His charmer took the packet from his hand and smilingly tore aside the wrapping.

"How lovely!" she exclaimed, as the bracelet was brought to view, and, with a delightful little courtesy, she tripped to the table and laid it among other remembrances of the joyous season.

He was permitted to lead his fair hostess into the dining-room, and was seated in the post of honor at her right hand. He could not help wondering, if this was a sample of her quiet dinners, what her large ones could be like. A gay lot were gathered around her hospitable board, and wine and wit flowed freely. The hostess and her companion, a prim little woman of about sixty, were the only ladies present. Either Mademoiselle's lady acquaintances were in the minority, or she preferred the companionship of the sterner sex. She did not leave the table when the wine was passed, but remained among her guests and partook of the sparkling glass as freely as any of those present.

Toast after toast was proposed and drunk before the signal was given for separating, when, instead of returning to the drawing-room, a rush was made for hats and coats, and in a few moments her guests, with the exception of Thomas, who remained to accompany her and her companion to the theatre, were seeking their various places of amusement for the night.

They were soon ready and on their way. Thomas was told off to escort the old lady to a box, while the actress disappeared behind the scenes.

When they arrived, the curtain had already risen, and our hero did not have long to wait before his divinity appeared on the stage. He amused himself between the acts by listening to the old lady's praise of her patroness, and searching the various tiers of boxes for the faces of some of his companions at the dinner table; but apparently they preferred the actress in private life, for not one of her guests, with the exception of himself, had paid her the compliment of being present this evening.

After the play was over, he was invited to supper in Mademoiselle's private boudoir; but her occupations had been too much for her during the evening, for she was tired and soon dismissed her companions.

Thomas was surprised, on getting out of a cab at the door of his lodgings, to see his rooms brilliantly lighted, and, hastening up stairs, he was about to enter the half-open door, when he discovered that his room was occupied. Stepping back, he peered in, and saw a group of seven or eight men gathered around the table in the centre of the room, at the head of which Mike was seated, dressed in one of his master's evening suits. A gay smoking-cap crowned his head, and a pair of light kids were drawn on his hands. The table was covered with glasses and decanters, and it was evident that his private stock of wine was pressed into service to help grace the festal board; but what was a greater surprise to him than all else, was to discover Sir Rupert and Lord Evelyn among Mike's guests.

Just as he made this discovery, his lordship proposed an adjournment. The rest of the company demurred at this; "but," said his lordship, "it would be awkward for Mike if Mr. Perkins should happen along and discover us all here."

"Oh! the fool will believe anything you tell him. We could soon trump up a yarn that would settle him. Throw a lord or lady into the discussion and he's a goner," replied Mike. "Can't we manage to present the actress as a duchess in disguise? It would bring him down in no time."

"I think you are doing pretty well as it is; but find out, if you can, Mike, what his resources really are. He may only have a temporary purse; but I think the supply is inexhaustible, for he is certainly too green to try anything in the way of speculation."

"I wonder if there are many more like him on the other side, Bill—or, begging your pardon, Mike. You'd better stick to the fellow, you might make all our fortunes."

"Yes, Mike," said Sir Rupert, "you might procure us each a big fruit farm out west. I wonder if picking apples is hard work."

"Too hard for this child, at all events," replied Mike. "We will run the Yankee greenhorn down to his bottom shilling, and then discharge him. We are not doing too bad. Mademoiselle has him fast, and we can take what she leaves. Well, gentlemen, I think you had better disperse. I want to lay aside my borrowed plumes before the peacock comes home to roost, and it will take me some time to turn into the meek and humble Irish servant."

"Do you ever get your Irish mixed, Bill?"

"Sometimes I stray into Scotland; but if it was Greek it would be all the same to that fool. He knows nothing except broken English, and a few scraps of American French, which some of the professionals on the other side of the Atlantic have managed to stuff into his obtuse brain. But off with you, for Mademoiselle won't keep him very late if left to herself; she is too indolent to exert herself, if there was a million in it."

Thomas stood spellbound, as he listened to this dialogue, until the whole thing flashed into his mind. He had been the victim of a gang of impostors. Yes! there was the pretended Lord Athol, who had given Mike a reference, among his guests. Well, he had been swindled out of something like a hundred and fifty pounds, but he had discovered them in time to get away before they reached his bottom shilling.

He decided that he had now had enough of English nobility, and would cross to the continent at once.

Advancing into the room, he startled them all by saying, politely:

"Good evening, gentlemen. I am sorry I was away when you came to visit me, but I see my servant has been doing the honors in my absence, and as he is dressed in one of my evening suits, I suppose that he answered as well as a Yankee greenhorn.

"Lord Athol, I believe. I hope you are not come to try and induce your old follower to return to your service, for I really have found him such a jewel that I could not possibly get along without him; and now, gentlemen, as the hour is late, I will wish you all a very merry Christmas, and bid you good-night."

"Mike, you can clear away that litter and bring me my writing-case."

As Mike did not obey this command, his master turned to repeat it, but found that he had disappeared.

"Ah! I presume that he has gone to lay aside his evening dress and resume his ordinary garb before returning to his duties. Excuse me, my lord, allow me to help you with your overcoat."

After the guests had departed, he rang repeatedly for Mike, but no Mike appeared. He cleared away the glasses and decanters himself, and, drawing a chair to the fire, tried to decide what he had better do now. Truly, England was not one of the most enchanting places in the world for a stranger! He would take the first opportunity of crossing to France. When he had arrived at this decision, he arose and sought his couch.

He was awakened the next morning by the ringing of the joyous Christmas bells. His first thought was of the happy family party gathered around the home fireside in far-away Nova Scotia. What would he not give to be with them to-day! There was no one in all this great city to wish him a merry Christmas! Well, he would amuse himself by getting ready for his journey to France.

How cold and cheerless everything was, when he entered his sitting-room; the empty grate and the scattered remains of last night's entertainment gave the place such a forlorn appearance, that, with a shudder, he went to call Mike. He found that gentleman had left with all his belongings, including the suit he had worn on the previous evening. He returned to the sitting-room, cleared the ashes from the grate, and soon had a cheerful blaze; he then began to look around for his breakfast, and at last managed to procure enough to satisfy his hunger.

After making the room as tidy as possible, he donned his outdoor garments and left the house. Remembering a former experience, when he had ventured alone in the streets of London, he remained near his door until he could obtain a cab to take him to his destination, which was the Great Western Hotel. Telling the cabman to wait for him, he walked into the office and asked for his letters. He received several, all bearing the home post-mark, the one from his mother containing a check for fifty pounds, as a Christmas gift.

After reading them, he began to prepare for his journey to Paris, and before night he was all packed and ready to start the following morning. He found, on consulting his landlord, that the pretended Lord Evelyn had taken his rooms for the winter; but, by forfeiting a month's pay in lieu of warning, he managed to get rid of them without further trouble. The next morning he left London at an early hour, firmly resolved to have nothing to do with strangers in the future, unless they were properly introduced.

CHAPTER XVI.

HAD Thomas followed his inclinations when he left his lodgings in the morning, he would have taken the train for Liverpool instead of Dover, and sailed for home; but he reasoned, "I came across the Atlantic to see Europe, and, as an eminent writer has said, 'In visiting Paris you see the whole continent.' I shall make a complete failure of the whole thing if I return now, and the poor mater would never survive the disappointment; besides, a fellow would have to stand any amount of chaff. So it is Paris or die."

With this heroic resolution he drove to the depot, and was soon on the road to the great European capital.

Purchasing his ticket, he found an empty apartment in the waiting train, and, entering, threw himself into a seat, arranged his wraps to his satisfaction, and began listlessly to watch the crowd outside.

Just before they started, he heard someone enter

the car and take possession of the opposite seat; but, true to his resolution of the day before to have nothing further to do with strangers, he did not even turn his head to look at his travelling companion. He amused himself for awhile by watching the changing scenery from the window of the now moving train; but, becoming tired of this after a time, he turned around, and, in doing so, glanced at his companion, who was sitting with his back partially turned towards him, occupied with a book. With a startled exclamation, he sprang from his seat, causing the stranger to turn his head.

"Can I do anything for you?" he asked, kindly. "Are you ill?"

"No, thank you," Thomas replied, "I was mistaken, that is all; I thought I recognized an acquaintance that I was not expecting to see, and I was for a moment surprised."

"I do not think that we have ever met before," said the stranger, with a smile, as he returned to his book, again turning his back upon Thomas, who sat looking at him for some time in perplexity. The figure was that of Lord Evelyn, and the voice not unlike his, but the face was that of a complete stranger; but, whoever he was, Thomas had no opportunity of making his acquaintance, for he appeared wholly taken up with his book, to the exclusion of everything else.

"Some cold, proud Englishman," thought our

hero, "who possesses a little money, and, because he happened to be born in an old stone house several hundred years old, thinks the world and everything it contains was made for his use alone. May the good saints protect me from ever having anything further to do with an Englishman; I hate the very sound of the name. They talk about the rascality of the Yankee, but for cold-blooded villainy commend me to an ordinary Londoner."

With this reflection, he arranged himself for a nap, but the rustling leaves of the stranger's book, as he turned page after page, prevented him from enjoying the repose which he sought. If he had only obtained a book before he started, he could have managed to make the time pass more pleasantly; but, he thought, "it takes time to get accustomed to the half-civilized ways of this country. If I was on a railway at home, now, and fancied a book, all I would have to do would be to seek the newsboy and get whatever I wanted; but who would want a book on one of our trains, where you could have the pick of perhaps a hundred people for a companion, instead of being locked into a cell with some unsocial English hog. I wonder how many hours more I will have to be penned here with him? If he was half a man, now, he would offer me that paper on the top of his gripsack; but let him keep his old trash, I shall buy a supply for myself when I get to the next news-stand. I wonder if there is any way to make them let you out of this hole before your ticket expires."

Just then the train stopped, and almost immediately after the guard entered the apartment and handed the stranger a telegram, and, receiving the customary half crown for his services, withdrew.

Thomas sprang to the door to call him, but he was too late. He pulled frantically at the closed door, but in vain, and, with a muttered curse on the customs of such a benighted country, returned to his seat.

"Did you wish anything?" now asked the stranger, glancing up from the book he had resumed.

"Yes; I wanted the guard to bring me a book, I cannot stand this sort of thing any longer," replied Thomas, savagely.

"I do not think that he would be able to procure you one now, before we reach Dover, even if you were to summon him; but here are some papers that may help you to pass away the time;" and, handing them over, he again turned his back and the next page.

Thomas took the offered papers, but could find nothing of interest in them. One was evidently a very popular sporting journal of the present day, while the other was devoted wholly to art, in neither of which was our hero interested.

After perusing them for a few minutes, he laid

them down in despair, and amused himself for some time in watching his companion turning the pages of his book as he read.

At last, with a sigh, he closed and laid it down in the seat. The ending was apparently pleasant, for the reader sat for some time after he had finished the volume, in a dreamy attitude, as if he was still wandering in fancy with the hero of the romance. Suddenly he turned to Mr. Perkins with the question:

"Do you object to smoking?"

"Not at all," was the reply.

He then produced a cigar-case, from which he took a cigar, closed it, and was about to return it to his pocket, when a thought seemed to strike him, and he offered it to his companion, with the question:

"Do you smoke? Would you care for one?"

"Thank you," said Thomas; "I was just longing for a good cigar. The fact is, I cannot get accustomed to your English ways of being forced to provide everything necessary for your comfort before starting on a journey. On our own railroads, when we want a book or paper, all we have to do is to wander through the train until we find the newsboy, and get whatever we want—books, papers, cigars, confectionery, or anything of the kind; and, indeed, we do not often have to go after him. About once in every half hour he takes a tour through the train, and you can order what you wish. It does seem so strange to me, after the freedom of an American railroad, to be locked into a little box like this, scarcely capable of containing a half dozen persons."

"You are an American, are you? I did not think that you had the appearance of an Englishman. The apartments on your trains are larger than ours, are they? And they do not lock the doors. I suppose the reason for that is in the maxim that 'in numbers there is strength.' If the savages, for instance, should happen to board your train, a body would be able to protect themselves much better than a few individuals; besides, you could make your escape more easily through unfastened doors. But it would not do in our country; there would be no privacy at all. We should be obliged to seat our most refined ladies by the side of some rough workman. I have read of the railroads in America. You have no exclusiveness there, rich and poor are mixed up together."

"We have our magnificent palace cars, where, if one does not mind the expense, he can travel as comfortably as if he was seated in his own drawing-room, with the ladies of the family around him. But the doors are not locked; tne conductor allows no intruders."

"It might do for America, but I hold it would not do for England. The Americans, I grant you, are a great people. I have just been reading an

American book, in which I was deeply interested. None except a Yankee could have ever formed such a plot in his brain. You are going to France, I presume. Do you intend to do Europe?"

"Yes; I am going to take a run over the continent for a pleasure trip. My name is Perkins, and I belong in Nova Scotia."

"I am happy to meet you, Mr. Perkins. They say confidence begets confidence. I believe I have left my card case behind; but you will find my name there," handing him the book he had been reading all the morning.

Thomas turned to the title page, and read:—
"To His Grace of Westmere, from his affectionate Eugenie."

"A live duke, and no fraud about it this time, for he is a perfect gentleman, and no mistake. He was not going to take any notice of me at first, but he found me irresistible. He is as reserved as all of his class, but I guess I can manage him. Ma knew what she was about when she sent me across the Atlantic. She knew I was bound to succeed. If Bill had been in my place, now, he would have taken up with that confounded Brown, and never got any higher. Now, if I can only get His Grace to go back to N. S. with me, who can tell what might happen. How it would tickle the old lady to be able to talk about my daughter, Her Grace of Westmere. How I could humble the Arlingfords when I meet them. Would I not enjoy telling them that I was just over for a short visit to my brother-in-law, His Grace of Westmere!

"If he was to see Janie, I know he would take a fancy to her; Janie is more like myself than Jule, and would stand the best chance. Jule is too old for him; but if we once secure His Grace, it won't take Jule long to pick an earl or viscount. I wonder if he has any sisters! They ought to be good-looking, if he has, or they cannot resemble their brother. If there are any, I shall try to catch one for myself. I am glad ma sent me that fifty pounds; I should not have been able to get along without it. I wish I had not been such a greenhorn as to give the actress that bracelet. I might have been able to dispose of it to one of the ladies of Westmere."

Here his soliloquy was cut short, for the train had glided into Dover, and the guard was unlocking the door of their apartment. His Grace had aroused from his nap, and was gathering his belongings together. Thomas followed his example, and in a short time the two were walking the promenade-deck of the Calais boat, and chatting as affably as if they had been comrades for years, and the determination of the day before to have nothing further to do with strangers, unless properly introduced, was for a time forgotten.

CHAPTER XVII.

REACHING Calais, Thomas could not help blessing the lucky incident which made the duke his travelling companion, for he soon discovered that his very American French was not likely to help him much, now that he had reached France; but His Grace, who appeared to be as much at home as if he was standing under the flag of Her Most Gracious Majesty, quickly extricated him from all his difficulties. A generous tip to one of the officials relieved him of the necessity of having his trunks examined, and the two called a cab and drove away.

"Your Grace did not seem to have any trouble at all with your own luggage. I suppose you cross so frequently that you are well known to most of the officials," said Thomas.

The duke laughed heartily, as he replied:

"No, I did not have any trouble with my own trunks, for the simple reason that I did not have any to bother me. I always find it less trouble to do without luggage when on a journey. One does not need to carry a complete outfit for a first-class tailoring establishment when going direct to Paris; you can generally manage to obtain the necessaries of life in that city."

"But, if you do not carry a trunk, what do you do with your clothes when you do buy them?"

"Wear them, of course; that is what they are made for, is it not?"

"I suppose so; but one does not always wish to remain in the same place long enough to wear out a suit of clothing. If you were in need of an evening suit, for instance, and went to the trouble of purchasing one, you would not be likely to wear it out in Paris, and if you had no trunk to put it into when you wished to leave, what would you do with it?"

"I should manage to rid myself of it in some way, if it became an incumbrance. Here we are at the hotel; prepare to be delighted with your first meal in France. If you are as hungry as I am, you will do ample justice to it. I could make a comfortable meal of the Russian bear this afternoon."

They went to the office, where His Grace registered their names and ordered luncheon. They were escorted to a private room by an obliging waiter, who showed them every attention. At the door the duke slipped a coin into his hand before they entered.

Thomas could not help thinking that it was a curious custom to be always feeing the servants, for he found that the bills had to be paid just the same. He had heard that in the old countries hired help was very much cheaper than in America, but for the future he would be inclined to doubt the statement.

In a short time a tempting lunch was placed before our travellers, to which they did ample justice. As the duke had predicted, Thomas was delighted with his first meal in France. Whether the pleasure of eating with a live duke, or the sea air, or the excellence of the cooking, had sharpened his appetite, he had never enjoyed himself so thoroughly at the table before.

He had read in ancient mythology of the ambrosial nectar sent to mortals by Jove as a Christmas gift, and he could almost fancy that France still retained the good graces of that ancient deity, and still received his favor at Christmas-tide, for the wine was something the like of which he had never tasted outside of French domains.

When they arose from the table, he insisted upon paying for the entertainment.

"Have your own way," answered His Grace, with a smile. "You Americans are so independent, that you cannot accept the least favor from anyone without making adequate returns. Well, I suppose we had better be moving, if we wish to reach Paris to-night."

"You are going to Paris, are you?" asked Thomas, delighted to find that he was still to have the benefit of His Grace's society.

"Yes; I might as well, I suppose, as I am on the road. I will go there for a day or two. The fact is, I was going to meet my sister, Lady Melville, who is wintering on the continent; but I received a telegram just before we reached Dover, informing me that they had changed their plans, and would remain in Italy for a few weeks longer. Although I have not seen her for some years, brotherly love is not strong enough to take me so far from home at present, so I shall return to England in a few days; but, as I have purchased my ticket, I may as well go to the end of my journey first."

In a short time they were again on the wing; but, on reaching the terminus, they found that the next train would not leave for nearly an hour.

The Duke took Mr. Perkins into the waiting-room, and asked to be excused for a short time, as he wished to take this opportunity of calling on a friend who lived a short distance away.

After His Grace left, Thomas decided that it would be as well for him to secure a stock of books and cigars for his use on the train. He pulled a small French dictionary from his pocket and hunted up the words that it would be necessary for him to use in asking for those articles, and wrote them on a piece of paper before committing them to memory. He then went to the news-stand and thus addressed the man in charge:

"*Vendre quell le livre.*"

"And who, in the name of common sense, is *Voder Quell?* And what can it matter to me whether he lives or dies?" asked that worthy in plain English."

I asked you to sell me some books, sir; but I supposed that you were a Frenchman, and, consequently, I addressed you in that language."

"I have heard of old English, but I never heard of old French; although, certainly, your pronunciation does not belong to modern times."

"Be that as it may, would it not be as well to drop the discussion and attend to the wants of your customer?"

"What shall I have the pleasure of getting for you, honored sir?"

"I have already asked you for some books."

"English or French editions?"

"English, if you have them," said Thomas.

"Here is a catalogue; choose for yourself."

Thomas took the proffered catalogue, from which he selected the names of four or five, ordered and paid for them, and walked away from the stall with all the dignity he could muster.

As he left, he heard the dealer remark to a companion that he would bet five to one that the idiot was some American cobbler's son, who was going to Paris to air his newly-acquired gold and scanty stock of French.

"He has been studying the language with some private tutor, probably, for the last three months, and is now going to the capital to perfect his pronunciation. They all do that as soon as they amass a little money. I can always spot one of them on the road, no matter how large the crowd."

Our hero waited to hear no more, but searched out the cigar stand, and this time asked for what he wanted in English; but he was not so fortunate here as to find any one who understood his language, and, not daring to repeat his carefully prepared French phrase, fearing to encounter further ridicule, he turned away in despair. After thinking for some time how to make himself understood, he pulled a pencil from his pocket, and putting the end of it into his mouth, he laid a piece of money upon the counter.

By this action the Frenchman understood that cigars were wanted, and immediately produced several boxes, from each of which our hero selected one and pushed the money towards him. At this the vender got very angry, and began to chatter in his own language, mixed with scraps of broken English; but the only word understood by Thomas was cheat. At last it occurred to him that more money was wanted, and, opening his purse, he handed him another piece, and the uproar quickly was stilled.

Just then the duke put in an appearance, and hurried his companion into the train, which was on the point of starting.

After they had arranged themselves comfortably in the apartment which had been assigned to them, His Grace asked what all the commotion was about.

"That foreign monkey behind the cigar stand thought I was trying to cheat him out of a penny," answered his companion. "I thought I understood the French language thoroughly. I had studied under some of the best professors in America; but here I cannot understand a word of their gibberish. Talk about the articles of the language, but my opinion is that the whole nine parts of speech are run into one gigantic combination."

"It does not seem to make a particle of difference how much one studies French," said His Grace, "you have to converse with a native of the country before you can make yourself understood. Did you get the cigars after working so hard for them?"

"Yes; will you have one?"

"Thanks! my case is quite empty, and I had not time to refill it on my return."

Each lighted a cigar, and lounging back in their seats, they were soon fast asleep.

They were awakened by the guard, who had

entered to light the carriage lamps, and, arousing themselves, were soon buried in their books, to the oblivion of everything until Paris was reached, and Mr. Perkins stepped from the train to gaze upon the great city in all her glittering glory.

CHAPTER XVIII.

THE next few days of Mr. Perkins' life passed away like a pleasant dream; the duke and he kept up a constant round of pleasure-seeking. He could not even find time for that glowing description of Paree, which his mother had asked for as soon as possible after his arrival; but he reasoned, as he put off writing the letter from day to day, "How can the dear old mater expect a description of Paris from me until I have explored the city?"

So he went on with his explorations, until, one day, exploring his purse, he found that the two hundred pounds with which he had entered Paris had dwindled down to a few francs. Then was the glowing description written and quickly started on its mission across the Atlantic, accompanied by an earnest appeal for more funds.

Scarcely had he dispatched his letter, when the duke entered and politely asked him for the loan of a thousand francs. Thomas was surprised, for it was only the evening before that His Grace had borrowed a thousand from him.

"You look somewhat surprised, my dear Perkins, at a duke being reduced to the necessity of borrowing money; but the facts of the case are these, the Westmere revenues are very small—a mere nothing for a man in my position; however, her ladyship of Melville backs all the unpaid bills, which are as numerous as the sands of the desert, for her good-for-nothing brother, as her old lord calls me. I expected, when I left home, to meet her on my arrival here, but her lord and master decided to remain in Italy for a few weeks longer, and keep his lady with him, so in consequence of my coming here almost penniless, I have written to her ladyship of my whereabouts, and will receive a draft in a day or two of several hundreds; but, in the meanwhile, I find it decidedly inconvenient to have an empty purse in a place like Paris. So, if you will be kind enough to accommodate me for a few days longer, I shall certainly remember you in my prayers."

Perfect silence reigned in the room for some time after His Grace finished speaking; but at length Mr. Perkins was obliged to confess, that, however much he might be willing, it was beyond his power to lend him the money.

"The fact is, my dear friend," he said, "on looking over my funds this morning, I was somewhat surprised to find that the two hundred with which I left England the other day, had melted down to almost nothing, and I have just sent a letter home asking for a draft to be sent at once. But, in the meanwhile, how am I to live? I suppose it will take nearly a month to receive the money. It was certainly very careless in me not to have made some better arrangement for supplying myself with cash on this side of the water before leaving home; but it never occurred to me that travelling in Europe would be so expensive. I had over two thousand dollars in my pocket when I left home."

"Why, my dear Perkins, you are indeed in a hard fix. Is there any danger of your people not honoring your draft?"

"No indeed! the money will be forwarded the instant my letter arrives; but how to exist in the meanwhile, is the problem to be solved."

"Well, if I was in your place, I should hunt out some cheap lodgings and lay low until the money comes to hand, and then, like a butterfly, emerge from your chrysalis. I will take a run across to England, after I see you comfortably settled, and look after my affairs there; and about the time your money arrives, Lady Melville will reach Paris, and we can all have a jolly time together. Her ladyship will get us into the first society of the city, so try and perfect your pronunciation all you can, and you will enjoy yourself all the more after your forced seclusion. Let us have a real good time tonight before we separate. What do you say to the opera?"

"Can we afford it, that is the question?"

"It will cost but a trifle, and you certainly want some pleasant memories to take with you into exile. I will go with you in the morning and help hunt up some cheap lodgings that I know of, where you will be comfortable, and, by paying for them in advance, you will secure a roof over your head for the next month. If you are careful, you can live on a mere nothing. You look surprised at my talent for economy; but, as I have already informed you the ducal revenues of the house of Westmere are almost nothing. I will have to pick up a city heiress some of those fine mornings, to fill my exhausted treasury; but I will wait until I exhaust the patience of my benevolent sister. A wife will be the last trump for me. I love my freedom too well to don the yoke as long as it can be avoided; but let us examine the financial department, and then away."

Thomas produced his purse, from which His Grace first secured a few five franc pieces for the evening's entertainment, and then proceeded to examine the contents in order to calculate on the month's expenditure.

After making a memorandum on a scrap of paper, he informed his companion that he would have about ten francs a week, after paying for his lodgings.

"You can exist very well on that in the quarters to which I shall take you in the morning; and now let us get ready for the opera," said His Grace.

The two were soon ready, and, calling a cab, they departed for one of the temples of amusement with which Paris abounds.

It struck Thomas as strange that His Grace, who had been existing, since their arrival in Paris, almost wholly at his expense, should make no calculation for the repayment of the fifty pounds obtained as a loan a few days before, and which he had promised to repay on the receipt of a draft from Lady Melville; but it would not do to ask him for it, for was he not a duke? and dukes, of course, were not pleased to be reminded of their indebtedness. However, he would try and manage without it until the expected help came from his mother.

The play was an interesting one, and the evening passed rapidly away. On leaving the building, His Grace called another cab, and they were driven back to the hotel.

After a late breakfast the next morning, which was served in their private room, the two went out together. Evidently His Grace intended to make it pleasant for his friend, as long as he could do so at the friend's expense, for he hailed a passing cab and they drove around the *Champs Elysées*, enjoying themselves among the glittering pageant as thoroughly as if their purses were filled to overflowing.

However, all things must have an ending, and the duke ordered the hackman to drive to one of the obscure streets opening off the *Rue Saint Quentin*, where he was told to wait for them at the door of a large but rather dilapidated-looking building.

A slovenly dressed girl answered the bell and the duke's inquiries. They were shown into a cold and bare-looking room, where they were soon joined by a coarse French woman of about fifty years, who addressed His Grace as *Monsieur Smeeth*. A short communication was carried on in French, and the duke told Thomas to follow them. The landlady led them up four or five steep and dirty flights of stairs, and at the top of the last she threw open a door and bade them enter. The room, though small, was quite clean compared with the rest of the house. The furniture consisted of a bed covered with a faded blue spread, a table, a washstand, a couple of chairs, and a small stove. A cracked mirror hung against the wall, and a torn curtain adorned the window.

Thomas could not help shuddering as he looked around, for he knew that this was the lodging that His Grace had promised to find for him; but how could the Duke of Westmere know of this vulgar Frenchwoman? and why did she address him as *Monsieur Smeeth?* Could he be an impostor, who was trying to pass himself off for the Duke of Westmere for some sinister purpose? But no, he drove away the suspicion almost as soon as it occurred; the man before him was too much a gentleman to impose upon anyone. Here he was, looking after his comfort in a strange city with as much kindness as if he was a brother instead of an acquaintance of a few days. He had acknowledged that he was poor; probably he had been at some time placed in the same position in which he now found his companion, and had thus discovered this place. If such were the case, was it likely that he would drag the ducal name of Westmere into a fourth-rate French lodging house? Of course not; that was how he was known to this woman by the name of Smith.

Just as he reached this conclusion, the duke asked him for his money; "For," said he, "I can settle this matter better than you, as I speak this crone's language."

After paying for the rent, Thomas found that he had very little left to provide himself with the necessaries of life for the next month; but his companion, who appeared to be possessed of the power of reading his thoughts, and observing the rueful glance he gave the almost empty purse, as he carefully placed it in his pocket, pointed to the gold coin dangling from his watch chain, and remarked:

"You can dispose of that if you get real hard up. British gold is current coin wherever you find it."

"I should not like to part with that," said Thomas; "for it was a gift from a friend when I was a little child, the first piece of gold I ever possessed."

The duke shrugged his shoulders, as he replied:

"As you please; but let us be moving, I want to catch the Calais boat. I told Madame Dufreè that you would take possession this afternoon."

They found the hackman waiting at the door, and they were soon on their way to the hotel.

"I suppose," said His Grace, after they seated themselves in the carriage; "that you were somewhat surprised to hear that old crone call me Smith, but I am going to pocket my pride and give you the plain, unvarnished facts. Last fall I came to Paris to meet Lady Melville, as usual. That is what I generally come for. And, of course, I came with an empty pocket; but, after getting myself established at the hotel where I was told to meet her, I received a letter informing me that his lordship was going to try St. Petersburg. A draft was enclosed to console me for my disappointment, but it had been sent in such a hurry that it lacked her ladyship's signature, so it had to be packed back to St. Petersburg to be ornamented with her autograph. In the meanwhile I had to exist, so I hunted out those lodgings; but, as I did not care to have it known that I was residing in such a place, I adopted the name of Smith. So, you see, I can speak from experience when I recommend the place to you. It will be rather dull, but the old girl will look after your comfort as if you were her own son; that is, if she thinks there is a prospect of getting well paid for her services."

They still kept the hack at the door while His Grace went into the office to settle their bill. When it was presented, even that gentleman's face fell. Horror of horrors! How in the world was the money to be raised? He went in search of Thomas, but soon found that the united fortunes of both were not sufficient to meet the bill. After much thinking, His Grace found a way out of the difficulty.

"You will have to leave your things here in security until we can raise the money. I will send it to you as soon as I obtain a check from my sister. In the meanwhile, slip a few things that you cannot do without into a valise, and let me take it with mine. I will see what arrangement I can make with the proprietor before I go."

In a short time they had everything arranged, and the two were driven to the station, where the duke took an affectionate farewell of his friend, and, promising to write frequently, stepped into the waiting train and was soon on his way to England. Before leaving, he ordered the hackman to drive Thomas to his lodgings, and they were soon on the way.

When they reached their destination, Thomas

handed him one of the ten franc pieces which his purse contained, which the man carelessly dropped into his pocket, sprang upon the box and whipped up his horses, leaving his fare standing alone and almost penniless on the sidewalk of a strange city.

CHAPTER XIX.

At length Thomas rang the bell at the door of the house which was to be his only shelter for the next month, and, being admitted, he toiled up the stairs to his room. A fire was burning in the grate, and a cup of cold tea and some dry toast was soon brought to him by the girl who answered the bell. Although he was very hungry, he could not help shuddering as he took the food from her dirty hands; but he quickly ate what she brought him, for he had not tasted dinner. He amused himself during the evening in arranging the few articles he had managed to bring with him. Among these was a small writing-case, and he decided that he could manage to pass away the next day in writing long letters to his sisters. He lay awake most of the night, trying to think of something to do that would make the month pass more pleasantly, and at last, thoroughly tired out, he went to sleep.

The monotony of his Parisian life was broken by an occasional letter from the Duke of Westmere, admonishing him to keep his spirits up in anticipation of the good time coming.

When he had been a resident of Madame Dufree's house for about four weeks, the anxiously looked-for letter from home arrived, containing a draft for two thousand francs, and accompanied by a letter from his mother, warning him to be more careful in the future, and be sure to save enough to bring him home, for, she wrote, "I had an awful time to get that from your father. Your sisters and myself will have to economize in every way for the next year to make it up. You ought to bring a duke home with you to repay them for the sacrifice they have made for you. You must have been fearfully extravagant to have put through so much money in so short a time."

After he had read the letter, he brushed his clothes and dressed himself as carefully as it was possible for him to do with the materials at hand, sent the girl for a cab, and went forth to cash his check. He inquired the way to the British consul's, and soon had his draft exchanged for the coin of the country ; then, like a boy let loose from school, he was soon on his way to his former hotel. He settled his bill with the proprietor, took charge of the keys of his trunks, and was once more established in his old apartments.

His first act after getting settled was to write to his friend, the duke, and give him an account of his changed fortunes. That worthy soon joined him, and the two resumed the life they had led when they first entered Paris together.

Following his mother's advice, Thomas carefully laid away the money needed to take him home, and with the rest determined to enjoy himself. Everything was going smoothly, and Lady Melville was daily expected. In the meanwhile, His Grace was living on Thomas's bounty.

One evening, about a week after the duke's arrival, Thomas lingered longer than usual at the *table d'hôte*. He had met a gentleman from New York at dinner, and the two were conversing agreeably when His Grace left the room. When Thomas reached their private room he was not to be found, so he went for a stroll in the grounds belonging to the hotel, while awaiting his return.

After walking around for a short time, he threw himself into a seat in a secluded part of the garden, and began thinking about home. The sound of voices in earnest conversation aroused him from his reverie, and he was about to move away when he heard his own name. The intruders had come to a stand a few feet from where he was sitting, and, looking through the shrubbery which concealed him, he was surprised to see the Duke of Westmere and his runaway London servant, Mike.

"I tell you, Ted, that I must have the money to-night," Mike was saying; "it's all very fine for you to say that you can't get it; but I tell you that you have got to get it. Perkins got a heavy check from home the other day, and will only be too pleased to lend the paltry sum of five hundred francs to His Grace of Westmere."

"I tell you it will not do for me to ask him for so much at once; you will have to wait. Even if he is one of the greatest fools in existence, he will be sure to suspect something wrong if I walk up to him and ask him for more so soon after his last loan. I am gaining his confidence as fast as possible, but don't expect too much from the fellow."

"Well, the money I have got to have, so get it as best you can. It is all very fine for Mr. Edward Smith to be the companion of the rich American, and have all his bills paid for him, and a good time generally, but the rest of us are not so fortunate. If there is a fancy job to be done, you always manage to secure it; but you must keep the rest of us afloat, too, if you do not want us to peach while you are playing the lord or duke."

Thomas waited to hear no more; but, like a flash, the whole plot was clear to him. The man who called himself the Duke of Westmere and Lord Evelyn were the same. He belonged to the gang he had found in his room on his return from the house of the actress on Christmas Eve. When they found that they were discovered, the pretended Lord Evelyn had disguised himself and followed him to

Paris, there to play the vulture until he had obtained possession of the greater part of his money. He had paid all the villain's bills for him since his return, but he had obtained no money from the second draft. Of course the fifty pounds were gone, but he had made the discovery in time to prevent being left penniless in Paris a second time.

"Good evening, gentlemen," said he, approaching them. "It is a beautiful evening for a stroll. Ah, Mike, I am pleased to meet you again. I presume you have come to return the suit of clothes which you accidentally carried off. You need not have taken the trouble, I will give them to you as a Christmas gift. It is customary, is it not, in this country, for people to remember their servants at Christmas? My Lord Duke, I will have to ask you to excuse me this evening, for I have important matters to attend to, and, as I suppose you will be returning to England immediately, I will say good-by here. Please remember me to your sister when you meet, and tell her ladyship to send the draft for the amount her noble brother owes me to my address in Nova Scotia, as I will probably return there before it is remitted; and, now, good-by. I suppose it is superfluous to add my good wishes for a very pleasant journey home, for how could it be otherwise than pleasant in the company of such an amusing person as our Irish friend, Mike? Besides, there is a chance of meeting a fresh victim on the road."

With this parting shot, Mr. Perkins turned on his heel and walked leisurely away, leaving the two conspirators looking at each other without the power of uttering a syllable. The pseudo duke was the first to break the silence.

"You see, you idiot, what you have done now!" he exclaimed, savagely. "You always have to upset our plans with your blundering. I told you not to come here, and now you see the result of your obstinacy. It is too bad! I expect that he had a good, big purse to empty. Well, staying here won't mend matters, so I may as well go and gather my belongings together and march. Meet me at the railway, we can do nothing more here; but it is as much as a bargain that I have money enough to take us both back to England, and of course you have made no provision for your return."

"Of that you may be sure, my hearty; I had all I could do to get here. But it will not cost a great deal to go third-class,—that is, if the great Duke of Westmere can come down to that, after all the splendor he has so recently enjoyed."

"Sarcasm is not your forte, try something else, my friend William; but you had better hurry, if you want to catch your train."

"All right, I am off; but give us a bob for cab fare."

"I have nothing to waste for cab hire. Walk, as you did when you came here."

"Very well, me darlint, I will remember you in my prayers,—as the good book says, 'An eye for an eye,' and so forth,—but don't try any of your games on me. If you do not turn up at the depot, I will have you before you leave Paris, as sure as fate."

"I have no intention of deserting you, much as I should like to do so, so be off with you."

The duke, or, as we shall call him for the future, Mr. Edward Smith, quickly laid his plans as he walked away. He knew that it would be useless for him to attempt any further disguise with Mr. Perkins. A man, be he ever such a fool, was not likely to be taken in a third time by the same ruse. "But," he reasoned with himself, "why should not Mollie have a chance to try her luck? He has never seen her, and it won't take her long to bring him down, and get a good handful of the ready. I will have to help fit her out, and it will not be much that I will get back; but I will have the satisfaction of emptying his purse to pay him for calling me a rogue."

He entered the house, obtained his valise, and started to meet his companion. He sent a telegram to the individual called Mollie, to meet him as soon as possible in Calais. He then joined his confederate, and buying a couple of third-class tickets, they went on board the train, where he turned his back on his companion and smoked his last cigar in sulky silence, until he went to sleep.

CHAPTER XX.

They reached Calais in the gray dawn of a cheerless February morning, where Mr. Smith gave his companion the slip after seeing him on board the channel boat. He returned to the hotel to wait the coming of Mollie, who soon put in an appearance.

"What will it be your pleasure to want with me now?" were the first words with which she greeted him when they met.

"Sit down, my dear Mrs. Smith, and I will explain to your ladyship. I have some work on hand for you."

"So I supposed, or I should not have been sent for. It is generally to do work that all others have failed to do that I am called upon. Whom have you been fleecing now? I hope you have left enough to make it worth my while to undertake the job; the last game you permitted me to take a hand in was not worth the candle."

"There is plenty in this, if you play your cards

us you well know how to play them. I hope you brought your jewels with you."

"You may be assured that I did not leave them behind me. I generally know what is wanted when I receive one of your affectionate little billet-doux; it is always to fleece some poor young simpleton, by playing the fine lady for his admiration."

"Have you brought Celine with you?"

"Why do you not ask me if I brought my bonnet and cloak? I should as soon think of starting without the one as the other. But you are a long time in coming to the point. If I did not know you so well, I should almost fancy that you were ashamed of what you are going to propose, you seem so fond of beating about the bush."

"Well, to be brief, then, there is in Paris at the present time, one of the greatest fools that America has ever produced, and that is saying a good deal. About Christmas the boys nearly cleaned him, out in London, but he discovered us and struck for Paris. I disguised myself and followed him there, and ran him to his last pound before I left; but he ordered a fresh supply from home, and went into retirement at old Dufree's until it came over, which it did about a week ago. I took such an affectionate interest in his welfare, that I crossed to France at once to give him the benefit of my advice, and help him spend it in a judicious manner; but before we got fairly at work enjoying ourselves, who should come along but that blundering fool of a Bill, and spoil the whole thing by insisting upon having a share of the spoils at once. The most unfortunate part of it was that Mr. Perkins (that is his name) overheard our little discussion, and called us a couple of impostors on the spot, although, previous to that, he had affectionately called me his dear friend the Duke of Westmere. So now, my dear, you are to finish him off and take his last penny from him; do not even leave him enough to pay the postage on a letter to Nova Scotia, asking for more money. I always want satisfaction when any one insults me."

"Would not the cheaper way have been to bring him up before a court for slander? What a base libel for any person to call such an honorable gentleman as Mr. Edward Smith an impostor! I can imagine your feelings. What heavy damages you might get!"

"You are pleased to be sarcastic this morning, my dear Mrs. Smith; but my honor should be yours also. I expect you to avenge my wrongs."

"As a loving wife should! Did I not promise to do so at the altar? Give me your commands, and I will obey at once. You have had my love for—how long? I forget the date. Now you have my honor and obedience. That makes up the catalogue, does it not?"

"You had better attend to my commands, then,

for time passes, and I should not like you to reach Paris, only to find the bird flown. You had better take a title; Mr. Perkins is a great lover of titles. Here is the money to defray your expenses, and you need no further instructions from me, so success to you, my dear. If you can manage to captivate the heart of the Nova Scotia millionnaire, he may take you home with him. You can amuse yourself in packing apples for the English market."

"And so relieve you of the burden of supporting me? Many thanks! I have no desire to be scalped by some savage while engaged in so delightful an occupation. I would much prefer the companionship of my loving husband in dear old England. But, good-by. I will report my success from time to time. I will call myself Lady Keating. If you have anything to communicate, you know the address."

Lady Keating, as she proposed to call herself, soon had her luggage and maid installed in the first train for Paris, and reached that city before dark, going direct to the hotel where Thomas was staying. She sent Celine to examine the books at the office, under the pretext of looking for a friend, whom she was expecting to meet there, and found that Mr. Perkins had not yet left.

She created quite a sensation in the dining-room with her elegant toilet, when she appeared at the *table d'hôte* in all the splendor of a blooming young widow just out of mourning for her gouty old lord. She soon recognized Thomas by his resemblance to a photograph which her husband had given her that morning, and managed to keep near him as he left the saloon, attracting his attention by dropping her handkerchief as she passed through the door. Thomas immediately secured it and presented to her, with his most gallant bow.

The smile and graceful little courtesy with which she acknowledged his politeness, almost turned that young gentleman's head, and although he had made up his mind to leave Paris for home on the following morning, he soon decided to remain and make the acquaintance of the charming stranger.

By careful inquiries of one of the clerks in the office who spoke English, he learned that she was a widow of high rank in England. The next morning he watched her door, which he found to be opposite his own, for her appearance at breakfast; but, after waiting for some time, he saw a servant bearing a tray, containing her breakfast, to her private room, and it was taken from her hands at the door by a smartly dressed French maid, who instantly disappeared. All day he hung about the corridor, watching for the appearance of her ladyship; but the hours passed away without his wish being gratified. He dressed himself carefully for dinner, arranged a flower in his button-hole, and went to the saloon soon after the bell rang.

He managed to obtain a seat near her ladyship, who was already at the table when he entered the room. As she was raising a glass to her lips, the clasp to her bracelet gave way, and it fell at his feet. As he handed it to her, she discovered that the portrait in the clasp was missing.

"Pray be careful," she said, "or you will tread on it. I would not lose it for all my wealth; it is a picture of his lordship, taken just before his death."

Assisted by a couple of waiters, they began a thorough search for the missing picture, but in vain. At last Thomas suggested that it might be clinging to her draperies, and, giving her skirt a shake, it fell from the folds. She gave a glad little cry as she raised it to her lips, and then carefully folded it in the belaced bit of cambric, which did duty as a handkerchief.

"Oh, thank you so much for your kindness! How can I repay you for the service you have done me this evening? That pictured face is all I have left of my dear old husband."

"Pray, do not mention such a trifle. I am only too happy to be of such slight service to so charming a young lady," replied Thomas.

"You scarcely seem a stranger to me. Have we ever met before?" asked her ladyship.

"I do not think so. I have only been in Europe a short time. I am Mr. Perkins, of Nova Scotia."

"Ah! a charming country, I have heard. I am

pleased to make your acquaintance, Mr. Perkins. My name is Lady Keating. It seems hardly the correct thing for a lady and gentleman to introduce themselves in the saloon of so public a place as a hotel; but no one except a gentleman would have taken the trouble to wait upon a stranger as you have this night, so I trust you will not consider me forward if I waive ceremony, and invite you to spend part of the evening in my sitting-room,—that is, of course, if you have no other engagement,—it is so lonely in this great hotel alone. I expect to meet friends in a few days; but, in the meanwhile, I have to fall back upon my own resources for amusement."

"I shall be most happy to accept your very kind invitation," answered Mr. Perkins, with his grandest bow; he had been practising it for the past month before the cracked looking-glass at Madam Dufreè's, and he now considered himself a master in the art of bowing. He offered his arm to the lady and escorted her to the parlor, where she brought all her powers of fascination forward for his sole benefit.

She played and sang for him for some time, and then proceeded to finish him with the magic of her brilliant conversational powers, which were far above the average. She gave a cry of surprise when the tiny clock on the mantle chimed eleven.

"Why, Mr. Perkins! where can the evening

have flown? I had no idea it was so late. You must excuse my thoughtlessness, and permit me to say good-night;" and, with a graceful bow, she dismissed him.

Thomas was delighted with the charming way in which she had given him to understand that it was time for him to leave, and he retired to dream of the wealthy and beautiful Lady Keating as his bride. He wondered if she would be able to keep her title, or would she be obliged to change it for plain Mrs. Perkins when he placed the golden circle on her finger.

CHAPTER XXI.

THE next morning he sent a carefully-written note to her ladyship, asking her to go for a drive, which invitation she accepted, promising to be ready in half an hour. The half hour brought Thomas in one of the most elaborate turn-outs that could be procured. He was in the seventh heaven of delight, as he drove with his fair companion around the city, she pointing out the historical places of interest along the route.

He spent the evening in writing about his prospects to his mother; he described the beautiful young widow as something almost too good for this world, but yet cherished the hope that when he arrived in Nova Scotia, she would accompany him as his bride.

For the next few days the pair were inseparable. They dined together at the *table d'hote*, they lunched together in her ladyship's private parlor, and always visited picture galleries and other places of interest in each other's company. A masked ball was to take place at the hotel, and the pair received cards of invitation.

This was what Mr. Perkins had been longing for ever since he had crossed the Atlantic; he wished to attend a genuine European ball.

After much discussion, he and Lady Keating decided to assume the characters of a Spanish prince and princess. In the course of the day, she informed him that she had ordered her dress, and the two waited with considerable impatience for the evening to arrive.

As he was reclining in one of the easy chairs in her ladyship's sitting-room the day before the event was to take place, Celine entered and handed her mistress a slip of paper, which she took with a slight frown.

"Mr. Perkins," she asked, turning toward Thomas and holding it in her outstretched hand, "can you tell me what is wrong with this? they have refused to cash it for Celine."

He took it from her, but his knowledge of the French language was too slight to enable him to decipher the writing.

Her ladyship placed it in her pocket with a resigned air.

"I will have to send it back to England to have the mistake made right, so good-by to the evening's pleasure. I cannot get my dress without money. Imagine Lady Keating having to stay away from a ball for the want of a dress to wear! What an item for one of the fashionable London journals."

"Have you nothing else you could wear?" asked Thomas, looking at the elegant silk in which her dainty form was then enveloped.

"Why, Mr. Perkins, of what can you be thinking? Did I not tell you this morning that I had not appeared in society since his lordship's death? So, of course, I have no dress I could wear. Any evening costume that I have would be over two years old. What a breach of etiquette it would be, to make one's appearance in a Parisian ball-room in a dress made two years ago! No, I will remain at home. I hope, some day, that there will be a uniform currency throughout Europe, so one can carry bank-notes from one country to another."

"Would it be too much of a liberty to offer you the money until your draft is rectified?"

"I must confess that I should hardly like to accept such an obligation from a stranger, or, pardon me, I should not have said that. It is very kind in you to make me such an offer."

"You need not consider it an obligation, and no one need be the wiser of the transaction."

"I feel strongly tempted to take advantage of your kindness, for I did want to go so much, I have led such a secluded life since my husband's death," and the dainty bit of lace she held in her hand was held up to her eyes.

"How much do you require?" asked Thomas, taking out his purse.

"I do not know; I will ask Celine," replied her ladyship, touching a call-bell on the table at her side.

Celine informed her that the dress was about one thousand francs.

Thomas was fairly aghast at this piece of information, and for a moment repented of his offer. It would take the most of his entire fortune; "but," he reflected, "it will be only for a few days, and I cannot refuse now."

"I have not the money with me, but will get it for you," said he, rising.

"Pray, do not put yourself to any trouble about the matter."

"The money is in my room; it will be no trouble, whatever, for me to bring it."

The money was soon placed in Lady Keating's hands, and Celine was dispatched for the dress, while Thomas went out to procure the flowers for the important event.

Dinner was soon over that evening, and, after dressing himself, Thomas went for her ladyship, to escort her to the ball-room. In his childhood he had often read descriptions of angels, but what pen could describe the vision of loveliness that almost dazzled him as Lady Keating stood before him? She wore a dress of some indescribable hue, draped with priceless old lace. Her neck and arms were sparkling with gems, and she carried a superb bouquet and magnificent jeweled fan.

"How do you like my dress, Mr. Perkins? Will I pass for a Spanish princess, do you think?"

"You would pass for an angel, if you only had the wings."

She laughingly tapped him with her fan, as she answered:

"No compliments, please. They are, at present, considered in bad taste. Let us go to the ball-room."

The evening passed away like magic, and everyone pronounced the ball a perfect success.

After a late breakfast the next morning, Thomas went to call upon her ladyship, and was admitted by Celine, who informed him that her mistress would soon be down. He picked up a book to amuse himself while waiting, and found an open letter between the pages. Before he had time to close the volume, his own name caught his eye, causing him to look more closely, and—good heavens! could he be dreaming?

"Dear Mollie," he read; "I hope you are fleecing that fool of a Perkins pretty freely by this time. I knew you would have no difficulty in making his acquaintance. Trust you for that. Well, all I ask of you is to strip him of his last penny. Do not even leave him the golden coin on his watch chain, which he prizes so highly, and you will have the eternal gratitude of your adoring husband, Ted."

Ted! the name by which Mike had addressed the man who called himself the Duke of Westmere! And so the charming young widow, Lady Keating, was that man's wife, sent to dupe him when her husband had been discovered. What enmity could they have against him, that made them so anxious to leave him penniless in a foreign city. She had, indeed, obtained the greater part of his money; but the gold on his watch chain yet remained. A rustle of silk caused him to look up, and Mrs. Smith, *alias* Lady Keating, stood before him.

"Good-morning, Mr. Perkins!" she exclaimed; "You are early—"

Thomas sprang to his feet, and indignantly pointed to the letter.

"Do you see that, Madam?" he demanded; "You should be more careful of your husband's letters, when you allow your dupe the freedom of your private rooms."

"I thought I had a gentleman to deal with, not a man who could descend to such depths as to read a lady's letters!"

"I have not been guilty of reading a *lady's* letters, Madam! I have only read the letter of an unprincipled adventuress! The end justifies the means. Will you have the kindness to return me the money I loaned you yesterday?"

"Certainly; as soon as my draft is cashed."

"That will probably be about the time your husband cashes some of those drafts of Lady Melville's. If your family were only as good at coining money as they are titles, you would all soon be rich enough to live without playing the vulture. Good-morning, Madam, you will hear from me in the course of an hour."

Thomas left the room after making this threat, but Mrs. Smith and Celine were on their way to London long before an hour had passed, and when he returned with an officer, a short time afterwards, he found the birds flown. He was soon packed and ready to follow them.

After paying his bill, he found that he had barely money enough left to pay his fare third-class to London.

Two hours afterwards he had shaken the dust, or, rather, mud of Paris from his shoes, and was on his way to England, where he hoped to obtain a chance to work his way to America in some homeward bound ship. He was completely cured of his love for titles; all he now asked from fate was the means to get home. His experience had cost him dear, but it would probably be the means of making a man of him. Henceforth he would be contented in the sphere in which Providence had placed him.

Reaching Calais, he soon had his luggage transferred from the train to the boat. He was very hungry, as he paced the deck of the steamer, for he had eaten nothing since breakfast time, yet he dare not spend the last money in his purse, even for food; but he concluded, "Of what use will French silver be to me in England, so I may as well get something to eat while I have the opportunity." Examining his purse, he found it contained a five-franc piece and an English shilling. He went to the refreshment stand and obtained a substantial lunch, giving the five-franc piece in payment, and now found his entire fortune was four shillings.

Poor fellow, he was indeed to be pitied! Alone in a strange country in the depth of winter, with scarcely a penny.

His eye falling upon the gold coin attached to his watch chain, it suddenly occurred to him that he might spend that, and go direct to Liverpool. "From there," he thought, "I shall stand a better chance to get home, for there are always more or less Nova Scotia ship-masters there who would be likely to help me." He detached the sovereign from the ring and placed it in his purse with a sigh. It was a childish treasure, that had been in his possession for years, and it seemed like parting from an old friend to lose it.

At length the long, weary night wore away, and the guard put out the carriage lamps just before London was reached. He had resolved to go direct to Liverpool; so, purchasing another third-class ticket, he was soon on his way. Lighting his last cigar, he fell back in his seat with a groan of despair. Until now he had kept his spirits up by smoking, but now even that comfort was to be denied him.

He arrived in Liverpool late in the afternoon, and sought a cheap boarding-house, where he could remain until he had the opportunity of sailing for America; and, once on the other side of the Atlantic, he felt that his troubles would be over, for he could walk home if no other way was open to him of reaching that desired haven. He soon found what he wanted, and, eating a hearty supper, he retired to rest, utterly worn out in mind and body.

CHAPTER XXII.

He awoke early the next morning, and, after partaking of a frugal breakfast at the nearest coffee-house, he started in search of a shipping-office. As he was inquiring his way, he met with a familiar face, which he instantly recognized as that of Bill Howard. He advanced with outstretched hand, but that gentleman declined now to recognize him.

"Serves me right," he thought, turning away with tears in his eyes, which were perceived by the sharp ones of the old sailor, causing him to instantly repent of his coldness.

"Tommy, what can I do for you? Are you in trouble?" he asked, hurrying up to him.

"Yes, I am indeed in trouble; I have lost all my money, and am now looking for a chance to work my way back to America. You are a sailor, can you tell me where I would be likely to obtain a berth in some ship?"

"You obtain a berth to work your way to

America! Why, you poor boy, they would be likely to leave you in mid-ocean! Yes, I can help you; but not in that way. I will lend you the money to pay your fare home, and you can give it to my sister Katie, when you have it to spare. Tell her I sent it to her for a Christmas present. She will think it has been all the time on the way."

"If I take advantage of your kindness, after the way in which I treated you on board of the *Vancouver*, I will tell her the truth."

"Come now, Tom, Bill Howard ain't the man to hold a grudge, especially agin Julie Smith's boy. I can spare the money just as well as not, and I should have sent something to little Katie long ago. Do you ever see her now? We used to call her your little sweetheart when you were children. I suppose she is a young woman now. Is she good-looking? It is over five years since I have seen her. She was a pretty little girl."

"She is called handsome," replied Thomas; "She is a dressmaker. I often see her, for she makes most of my sisters' dresses."

"I suppose she is not invited to the balls and parties that I have heard your mother gives."

"No; to tell you the truth, she is not; but she will be for the future, if I can manage it, of that you may be sure."

"That is right, be good to poor little Katie, and

it is all I will ask. We will go to the agents' and see when the first steamer sails for home."

They found the first steamer left in three days, and, after considerable discussion, a place was taken for Thomas on board. He was determined to take a passage in the steerage, but in this he was overruled by the old sailor, who insisted upon his going in the style in which Bob Perkins' boys were accustomed to travel. At last a compromise was made, by which he went as a passenger in the second cabin.

After that matter was disposed of, Mr. Howard proceeded to do the honors of Liverpool for the benefit of his young friend. The first place to which his guide led him was a whiskey saloon; but imagine the astonishment of the old sailor, when Thomas refused to partake of his hospitality in the form of whiskey.

"Don't you drink anything at all? You would like a glass of wine, maybe."

"No, I thank you; I never touch intoxicating liquors."

"That's right, my boy! Give me your hand. I might have known that Julie Smith's son would soon turn right side up, although I own I was awful mad when I met you on board of that boat, and you pretended that you didn't know me at all."

"I acknowledge that I was wrong, and I hope you have forgiven me; but you must own that it was not pleasant to be told, in the presence of a charming young lady who despised the very name of trade, that my mother once sold eggs for a living."

"I suppose not; but what became of the charming young lady? Sent you adrift when she got all your money?"

"No, she did not get my money, but she sent me adrift when she found that I had to work for a living. A gentleman calling himself the Duke of Westmere borrowed all my money, and, after he got possession, I found that he was too poor to give it back, so I got left. Although such gentry are too proud to work, they are not too proud to spend what other people work for; but let us talk of something more pleasant."

The three days soon passed away, and Thomas took an affectionate farewell of his friend on the deck of the *Sarnia*. He neglected to ask the name of the ship he was to sail in, and the last two days of his stay in Liverpool were somewhat spoiled, by his thinking that it might be the *Vancouver* in which he would have to cross; but what was his joy, on reaching the ship that morning, to find that it was the *Sarnia*. When he left, he made Howard promise to write to him frequently, and also to come home and see them all before long. This the sailor promised to do, and they parted with real regret on both sides.

The homeward voyage was uneventful, and the

steamer dropped anchor in Halifax harbor the ninth day after leaving Liverpool. Thomas soon had his luggage examined, and went to a modest hotel for the night, for he had arrived too late to take the evening train for home.

He reached home the following day just as the family were seating themselves for the early dinner, which the elder Perkins always insisted upon, regardless of the protests of his wife and daughters, who fain would have dined at a more fashionable hour. He was received with open arms, although it was quite a disappointment to the female members of the family to have him return with neither lord nor duke in his train.

CHAPTER XXIII.

Mrs. PERKINS was for celebrating the traveller's return by giving a grand ball, but she was overruled by Thomas. Mr. Perkins was so delighted with what he considered his son's good sense, that he presented him with a fifty dollar bill on the spot. Poor old man, he had learned by bitter experience, that the best way for him to show his affection for his family, was to provide them with plenty of money.

Thomas thanked his father warmly for his gift, and informed him that for the future he should like to depend upon his own exertions, for he considered that he had wasted enough of his parent's money.

The old gentleman was so pleased at this piece of information, that he told his son that he considered the money was well spent if it had procured him a little sense; "for you must own that you needed it bad enough when you started for France," he said.

"I must acknowledge that I had rather romantic

ideas," said Thomas; "but knocking around a bit has boiled them down. If you can help me to get a situation, I shall only be too glad to go to work now."

"What would you like to do? Your ma wants you to make a lawyer of yourself; she says that you would be an ornament to the profession."

"Right she is, there, as the dear mother always is. I should be an ornament to the profession, but of no earthly use there. I am afraid that jurisprudence is not my forte. I should much prefer being a clerk or book-keeper in some office."

"Is that so? Then I know just the thing for you. Old Brown, down to the station, wants a clerk; so, if you would like the place, I can get it for you. I don't suppose there is much money in it, though."

"Enough to supply my simple wants; so, if you can get the situation for me, please secure it at once."

If Mr. Perkins was pleased at what he called his son's good sense, he soon found that his wife was not so easily satisfied.

"To think," she said, "after all the money they had spent on him, trying to make a gentleman of him, that he should want to go into that dirty little railway office! Why, he has lost what little sense he had before he left home! If he wants to do something, why doesn't he study law? I always intended him to be a lawyer."

"But the boy thinks that nature did not intend him for that profession."

"Nature intended him for an idiot! I think he will end by marrying some low-bred girl, and turning farmer. It was only last night I actually saw him walking up the street with Kit Howard, the girls' dress-maker. Just think of it!"

"I should not advise you, Mrs. Perkins, to repeat that where the Howards would be likely to hear it, or they might retaliate by saying that Katie was walking with the son of people who were once their servants. You forget that we were not always rich. For my own part, nothing would please me more than to see Thomas marry Katie Howard. I consider her a very sensible young woman; and if he wants a farm, I shall only be too glad to get him one."

"It will break my heart to see him come down to that, after all my hopes."

"I do not think there is any danger of that. You can take the girls and start for Paris before the wedding comes off. I would not mind the cost of another tower this year, if it only ended as satisfactory as Tom's has.

"I should enjoy that. When does the happy event take place?"

"I have not been informed of the date, but soon, I should say, from what Tom told me to-night."

THE END.

www.ingramcontent.com/pod-product-compliance
Lightning Source LLC
Chambersburg PA
CBHW022115160426
43197CB00009B/1041